INTRODUCTION

Several years ago, Guideposts selected Emily Gardiner Neal's great book, *God Can Heal You Now,* and offered it to our readers. The editors chose it because they believed it offered practical help and rare insights into the often beclouded subject of spiritual healing. Mail soon bore out our opinion as many wrote to tell us how much they had been helped by Mrs. Neal's words. Since that time her writing ministry has further grown until today she is recognized as one of the world's outstanding commentators on the subject.

When we learned of Mrs. Neal's new book, *The Healing Power of Christ,* we immediately asked the publisher to send advance proofs to us. We read again the exciting and continuing story of how God's healing power is at work today, and before we had finished the manuscript, we knew again that we wanted to share this book with the Guideposts audience. Mrs. Neil's good news is that there are more healings taking place today than at any time in her long healing ministry.

Illustrated with case histories of all types of healings, Mrs. Neal does more than report them, she comments about the conditions that figured in the blocking or restoration of health. Furthermore, Mrs. Neal talks about her own recent physical suffering—how she lived with it, how God answered her prayers and healed her and how this experience led her into a deeper relationship with Christ.

People in need of spiritual or physical healing will find this book a unique one, full of compassionate wisdom and uplifting truth. It cannot help but inspire and encourage thousands who have yet to experience the healing power of Christ.

The second half of this 2-in-1 Guideposts selection is Bruce Larson's popular, *Dare to Live Now,* a lively art of living book which challenges each of us to make more of every moment God gives. Honest, practical, anecdotal, refreshing, Bruce Larson cuts through the maze of problems which tend to sour and immobilize people today and offers a solution: the joy and power that comes from serving Jesus Christ. If for example, you want to break out of a rut, or change a bad habit, or restore a broken relationship, or eliminate destructive thoughts, you will find plenty of ammunition herein to deal with the problem.

An enthusiastic book with a dynamic message, no one will put this book down without receiving some personal help and direction. Furthermore, Bruce Larson writes with a zest that makes him fun to read.

Both *The Healing Power of Christ* and *Dare to Live Now* are books that could revolutionize your life. The application, of course, depends on you.

—The Editors

The
Healing Power
of Christ

EMILY GARDINER NEAL

Dare
To Live
Now!

Bruce Larson

GUIDEPOSTS ASSOCIATES, INC.

Carmel, New York

The
Healing Power
of Christ

EMILY GARDINER NEAL

GUIDEPOSTS ASSOCIATES, INC.
Carmel, New York

Guideposts edition published by arrangement with
Hawthorne Books

This book, written for the glory of God, is dedicated to the Reverend Donald Turley James, great Christian, faithful Episcopal priest, and beloved friend.

The scriptural passages quoted in this book are from the King James version unless otherwise noted. The abbreviations of other translations are as follows:

B.C.P.	Book of Common Prayer
Jer.	Jerusalem Bible
N.E.B.	New English Bible
Phillips	Phillips translation
R.S.V.	Revised Standard Version

Foreword

MY FIRST BOOK, *A Reporter Finds God*,[1] conceived when I was an agnostic, was intended to be an exposé of "faith healing." As I researched the subject, however, I was myself converted, and the book was to end as an apologetic for the Christian faith in general and the healing ministry in particular.

Since that first book, others have followed as I have watched the ministry of healing spread from what, just a few years ago, was considered an esoteric practice, confined to a few churches (mostly Episcopal) to hundreds of churches of virtually every denomination. In these churches it is acknowledged for what it is: a scripturally founded ministry following the commandment of our Lord to preach the kingdom *and* heal the sick (Luke 9:2). It is a ministry that accepts Jesus' revelation of a God who wills the complete wholeness of body, mind, and spirit for His children; a ministry practiced by the ancient church in obedience to Christ's imperative; a ministry that almost died out after the third century; a ministry that has been revived today and in which we see manifested much of the spiritual power of the early church as we observe ailing bodies marvelously healed and sick spirits restored to wholeness.

Over the past years I have become increasingly in-

[1] New York: Morehouse-Gorham, 1956.

volved in the ministry of healing until it now consumes
not just a major portion of my time, but my entire life.
I have led innumerable healing missions in churches of
every denomination throughout the United States and
Canada, and only lack of time has prevented my accepting invitations to Europe and Australia.

Since 1966, at the invitation of the rector, the Reverend
Dr. John Baiz, and with the permission of my bishop, I
have had the privilege of leading weekly interdenomina-
tional healing services at Calvary Episcopal Church in
Pittsburgh. These are always conducted in participation
with a clergyman. Believing as I do that the healing
ministry must be kept within the church if it is to be pro-
tected from chicanery and the excesses of misplaced zeal,
I work always under the authority of my church. As my
deepest desire and chief purpose is to see the establish-
ment of healing ministries in every church, the work at
Calvary has been enormously gratifying, for as a result of
these weekly services, numerous clergy of different denominations have begun healing services in their own
churches.

More healings are occurring today than at any time
since I have been associated with this ministry. This is
particularly evident in regard to cases of acute leukemia.
For years it was virtually impossible to procure reliable
documentation of this disease. Over the past few years at
Calvary and during missions, I have seen numbers of
such cases diagnosed as "acute" where the life expectancy
was estimated to be very short regardless of possible
remissions and the administration of new drugs.

By means of concentrated prayer, the sacramental healing rites, and holy communion, remissions have occurred,
many of them of such long duration that it seems reasonable to suppose that cures have been effected. In my
experience the reception of holy communion in this disease—and indeed in all blood disorders—is of supreme

importance. There is a close relationship between the Blood of Christ shed for us and that received by us in this sacrament, cleansing, healing, and mystically coursing through the veins of the supplicant. No matter how young the leukemia victim, I urge frequent communions.

In ever increasing number we see the crippled walk, the blind see, and the deaf hear. We see the retarded restored to normalcy, the emotionally and mentally sick healed. We see brokenness of all kinds, in every area of life, healed. And in the area of unbelief, which constitutes the greatest of all brokenness, we see the greatest of all miracles as the faithless are brought to Christ.

"Hitherto have ye asked nothing in my name," Jesus says. "Ask and ye shall receive, that your joy may be full" (John 16:24). We have asked, we have received, and we know well that joy of which He speaks.

As you will note throughout this book, the healing ministry is in no way confined to physical illness; it touches every area of our lives. The healing Christ extends His hand to bless, to heal, to bring us to Him. The ministry of healing, although only one of the ministries of the church, serves in unique fashion to open our hearts to the love of God. At the altar rails of the healing church, Christ is overwhelmingly present, and there is an almost startling awareness of Himself and of His love which *is* Himself. It is this awareness that enables us to meet and conquer two of the major problems confronting not only our youth but individuals of every age: the apparent meaninglessness of life and the agonizing search for self-identity.

As we discover with impelling impact through the healing ministry that Christ does indeed live today, we find in Him the meaning of our lives. In our subsequent commitment to Him we find new purpose, for we know at last the reason for our being. In regard to the so-called identity crisis, we recall the words of Saint Augustine:

"Let me know Thee, Lord, and let me know myself." It is in knowing God that we come to know ourselves as His children. For me and for many, this is enough. We know at last who we are and why. Our search is ended. We are found.

Properly understood, the healing ministry is not a ministry of self-gratification. It extends far beyond the needs of the individual or those close to him. It involves itself deeply in the world's suffering. Those associated with this ministry do not dwell in ivory towers. They attempt to follow the precepts of our Lord, fully aware that they are His hands and feet in this world, cognizant that as the body without the spirit is dead, so faith without works is also dead (James 2:26).

This book is the continuing story of the healing Christ at work among us today as surely as he was present among the people two thousand years ago. It tells of some of the marvelous healings of every kind in the lives of twentieth-century men, women, and children. In order to avoid what might be an undesirable identification with any particular church or mission, I have intentionally "scrambled" the healings and other happenings recorded. For example, where one particular episode occurred which could be identified with one particular mission, I have included in this same mission, stories and case histories which in fact occurred elsewhere—many of them at Calvary in Pittsburgh. The important thing is that everything reported happened under the circumstances described.

As the book relates wonderful healings wrought by God, so does it tell of the no less wonderful way in which He uses suffering as we await our healing. Suffering as well as healing is now rooted in my own experience, and it is the sharing of this suffering that makes this book unusual. Many people actively engaged in the healing ministry attempt to keep knowledge of their illnesses from the public, no doubt feeling that if it is generally known that they have not received instantaneous healing, the faith of others in the healing Christ may be damaged. From my observations, I do not believe this to be true. On the contrary, I have seen the hope and faith of the vast majority strengthened when they learn that even a leader in the healing field is not always immediately physically cured, but that in the strength of Christ he is enabled to go on in the unshakable conviction of God's will and power to heal.

For years I felt presumptuous when from the pinnacle of my own extraordinarily good health I would say to the suffering, " 'Seek ye *first* the Kingdom' is the master key to healing. You must seek God for Himself and not just His healing gifts. Therein lies your best hope of physical healing." I no longer feel presumptuous in saying these words, and I know their validity as I never fully understood before. I have had to apply them to myself, because for a period of nearly six years I was never a day without pain, and had it not been for the strength of Christ in which I walked and worked, I would have been totally incapacitated from a spinal injury suffered in 1965. Although for years there was no evidence of healing in my own body, I feel myself not less blessed, but more—for I have known His grace in my life to an extent I never knew before, continually sustaining, enabling and empowering.

While I no longer feel hesitant in asking the suffering to seek God for himself alone, I do not underestimate the difficulty of this undertaking. I realize that there are times when pain supersedes all else; but I also know that there are times when the pain, no matter what the ailment, is less. God in His mercy requires only a moment of complete relinquishment to Him to work a miracle.

Some of my beloved friends, without whose prayers I could not have continued, have said to me in real distress, "But why should *you* have to suffer so?" Deeply grateful for their concern, I was nevertheless upset myself by this question because they were upset. The answer seemed to me so clear: Why *not* I? Everyone on earth is subject to suffering, and why should I be immune? To be a Christian is not an insurance policy against the coming of disaster; it is rather assurance against being overcome by it—for no matter what happens to us, we hold in our hearts the joy of the Lord, submerged at times by pain or adversity, but always deep within our beings. We may indeed suffer, but He was crucified and yet rose again. No matter what happens to us, we know that beyond the Cross lies the Resurrection. In this knowledge lies that joy which cannot be taken from us.

It seems to me a sort of blasphemy to castigate God by the querulous question, "Why?" It is only when we learn to stop this needless questioning that we feel impelled to offer Him endless praise and thanksgiving simply because He lives and because we know it; because He is with us and within us every second of the day and night; because He heals, and we experience His healing; because He loves, and we are the objects of His love; because *with* Him all things are possible, and *in* Him lies our hope, our joy, the reason for our being.

I have been blessed by my friends and am grateful beyond the telling for their love, concern, and ceaseless prayer. I have been deeply moved and inexpressibly thankful when during many missions and at the Calvary services total strangers learning of my physical difficulty have surrounded and upheld me by prayer.

I thank God for my Christian family physician, for his medical skill and for his belief in the power of prayer. Throughout the years he never relinquished hope of my healing, despite the verdict of orthopedists, neurosurgeons, and doctors of physical medicine, whose common opinion was that I should stop working and learn to live "with a physical condition which in all probability would worsen with time."

Finally, no words of mine can adequately express my gratitude to God for the late Reverend Donald T. James, director of the Pittsburgh Experiment, who ministered to me faithfully as I struggled to keep going. He gave unstintingly of that love, divinely bestowed, which he possessed to so extraordinary a degree. And God worked through him to heal in the way that mattered most.

At the end, Don was to give me the gift I treasure above all others in this world: the privilege of ministering to him after his first heart attack. The year following was one of mutual ministration for which I shall always be grateful: a year of joy, of healing, of singular closeness to one of the great Christians of our time.

"Call unto me, and I will answer thee, and show thee great and mighty things, which thou knowest not" (Jer. 33:3). This is the promise magnificently fulfilled in His ministry of healing.

E.G.N.

Contents

Contents

"By the bruising of my whole life, strengthen me with sympathy for every wounded soul, and let my prayers be as balm for the wounds of Thy children, that they may be healed."
—Dorothy Kerin, *Called by Christ to Heal*

Chapter 1

THE LONG
ROAD BEGINS

GLANCING AT MY watch, I noted that within half an hour the plane would be arriving at my destination—a city far from home—where I was to lead a three-day healing mission. The stewardess was serving coffee to the passengers, when the plane hit rough weather. I smiled to myself at the seemingly inevitable simultaneity of air pockets and coffee-serving. As the "Fasten Seat Belt" sign flashed on, I started to reach out for my cup but quickly changed my mind. The plane was pitching and plunging too much to risk a shower of hot coffee. The stewardess, undaunted, walked past me, struggling to keep her balance.

As the plane hit another air pocket I tightened my seat belt, and at that moment a small child, sitting a few seats in front of me, escaped from his parents and began to run up the aisle. The plane gave a lurch and the child started to fall. Instinctively I twisted quickly in my seat to catch him. That sudden movement of my body, confined as it was by the seat belt, wrenched my back in such searing pain that I thought I would faint.

At the time of the initial injury to my back, six months earlier, I had had to cancel one mission, fortunately the last of that season and the first I had ever had to cancel. It had been a difficult summer of lying flat on my back for weeks on end, but by the grace of God I was up and around once more, and had recently completed several missions. As I sat in my plane seat now in excruciating pain, I could only pray; "Lord, if I am to do this mission, You'll have to make it possible."

The plane landed, and with superhuman effort I got myself down the ramp, where I was met by the smiling rector of the mission church, who was full of plans for the mission which was to begin the next day. I said nothing about my back until we arrived at the hotel where I was to stay. Unable to get out of the car, I was forced to tell him what had happened.

I will long remember his kindness. Instead of being upset over the probable cancellation of the event planned two years before and widely publicized, his sole concern was for me. After a short prayer, he called a physician who, after a cursory examination, said that I must be hospitalized at once.

"But what about the mission?" I asked.

"Forget it," was the response. But this was an unrealistic order, for how could I "forget" it when I knew that busloads of people were arriving from far-distant points, that hundreds would be bitterly disappointed, and that there was no time to procure another missioner?

Early next morning while I was still groggy from Demerol, the physician and rector stopped by my hospital room. Before either could speak, I said, "I'll do the mission." The physician demurred but was understanding albeit skeptical.

"All right," he said, "if you think you can. But of course you'll have to return to the hospital immediately after each session. Have therapy as often as possible, and we'll try to keep you free from pain."

An hour before I was to leave for the church for the opening service that evening, three nurses came in to dress me. A back brace had been hastily fitted, and while one nurse was strapping me into it as I lay on the bed, another was pulling on my stockings. The third nurse stood by my head and said, "Mrs. Neal, please don't try it. You'll never make it."

I knew better than anyone that I could never make it on my own—but I also knew that I could "do all things through Christ which strengtheneth me" (Phil. 4:13).

When I was finally dressed but still lying flat, the physician came in with a packet of pain pills. "Take one of these now," he said, "and carry the others with you. You can sneak one into your mouth as you take a sip of water from the pulpit."

I refused the pills, afraid to take them lest they befuddle my mind, and the physician left the room.

To my surprise and joy, the nurses stood around my bed, and one of them said, "We'd like to pray for you before you go." Deeply grateful and greatly strengthened, I managed to get off the bed, and I was taken to the church.

As I stepped into the pulpit, the first person I saw was the kind physician, who had taken time off to come to the service; he was waiting to catch me if I fell. However, stronger hands than his were to hold me up that night.

The church was packed, and only the rector and I were to administer the laying on of hands. According to usual custom we divided the altar rail, he taking one half and I the other.

The line of people streaming up to receive the healing rite seemed endless. Each time I finished my section of the rail, I turned toward the altar with the silent prayer, "Lord, let Thy strength be made perfect in my weakness." Little did I know that night that this would be the burden of my prayer for years to come, as during mission after mission I could not under my own power stand on my feet.

By the time the last group came up to receive the laying on of hands, I had been standing for nearly four hours, and I could scarcely walk. Reaching down to hang on to the altar rail, I suddenly felt a firm hand under my left elbow and then an arm around my waist, which held me up straight and strong until the last supplicant had been ministered to. The service over, I slipped out the back door and into the waiting car which returned me to the hospital.

Next morning the rector telephoned and I thanked him for supporting me at the rail the night before. With some embarrassment I felt compelled to add, "I certainly needed your help last evening, as I was about to collapse, but tonight could you please get us more clergy to help with the laying on of hands? I managed last night because you held me up and I am grateful, but please don't do it again. It seems hardly suitable at a formal service to have you with your arm around me supporting me!"

There was a long silence at the other end of the telephone—and then, in a small voice, came his words: "Emily, I didn't touch you during that service. I was finished before you, and during the last fifteen minutes I was kneeling before the high altar."

Then I knew: Not only had Christ upheld me, He had quite literally held me up. And so it was to be in the years that lay ahead. At home I was unable to stand for the reading of a psalm, but during a mission I was on my feet for three or four hours at a time, solely in His strength.

During this mission there was a great outpouring of the Holy Spirit, and many healings were reported. The only obligation I could not fulfill was that of greeting people after the services. If the time between the various daytime sessions was short, the rector would take me to his study, where with the door locked I lay on the floor (my back needed a hard surface) until time for the next event. Again, little did I know that for months and years to come, I would have to rest on the floor of the clergyman's study in whose church the mission was being held. I am sure my record is unique in one respect at least: Never has anyone lain on the floors of so many pastors' studies!

I was in the hospital for some days after the mission, during which time several prayer-group members came to visit me. This was a surprise, as I was unaware that anyone other than the clergy knew I was there. As I look back now, it was actually these kind women who sowed the first seeds for this book. One said to me, "Why didn't you let us know your predicament so we could have been praying for you?" My only answer was the true one: It had never occurred to me to tell these people, and I could only wonder why it had not.

The love and concern of these prayer-group members, and the letters I received later, demonstrated once again how God can use any and everything for His glory. Typical of these letters was one which read: "I was miserably ill last week—and then I remembered your doing that mission in the strength of Christ. What an inspiration, as through you we saw the living Christ sustain and enable. Suddenly my own sickness seemed very trivial, and God healed me in record time."

It was recalling letters like this that caused me to believe that for others as well as myself the visible evidence of the enabling power of the Holy Spirit was as great a miracle as a physical healing.

Before leaving the hospital, the physicians urged me to cancel missions scheduled for the immediate future.

Rather than canceling them, I rescheduled them for the following fall and winter. This made an exceedingly heavy schedule for the year ahead. I did not dream that I would not be perfectly well by then. Yet, despite frequent further injury, by God's grace I have never had to cancel or even curtail another mission—nor have I ever been obliged to miss a healing service at Calvary.

On the basis of my own experience, I am amused as I think of the lengths to which many of us who work in the healing ministry go in our attempts to explain away Saint Paul's thorn in the flesh (II Cor. 12:7).

I myself have done this often, both in former books and in public speaking, for in years gone by, people would often ask: "But what about Paul's thorn? If *he* wasn't healed, how can *I* expect to be?"

The answer I invariably gave was, first, no one really knows what the apostle's thorn was. The phrase is used in three other places in the Bible (Num. 33:55; Jos. 23:13; Judges 2:3), and in no case does it relate to physical illness. Therefore Paul's thorn may well have referred not to a physical infirmity but to a spiritual one, such as pride.

Whatever Paul's thorn, it was apparently eventually healed, for in Gal. 4:13 his infirmity is referred to in the past tense.

All this is true. However, when people occasionally still say to me: "But what about Paul's thorn in the flesh?" my reply is: "Well, what about it?" It seems to me now to matter not at all. There are only two things in connection with it which seem of importance:

First, whatever it was, it was not of God. "There was given me a thorn in the flesh, the messenger of Satan to buffet me," Paul says (II Cor. 12:7).

Second, the all-importance of God's answer to Paul when he prayed that the thorn be removed: "My grace is sufficient for thee, for my strength is made perfect in weakness" (II Cor. 12:9). And so it was. The apostle was enabled to do the will of God and in the process to endure stonings, shipwreck, and persecution. No matter what Paul suffered, it did not impede his work, for Christ was always victorious.

So it was during this mission led from the hospital, and so it would be in all the missions to come for a long, long time. I thought often of St. Paul, and drew courage from his example.

There was not a day during these years that I did not expect and claim the miracle of physical healing in my own life. As time after time I received the healing rites, at a point at which I felt I could bear no more suffering, the pain would marvelously cease. I would be certain then that the healing had occurred—and so, for the moment, it had. But for reasons I did not know, I could not hold it. Within a short while, the pain would be back; but it was as if by each easement of the pain God was reassuring me of His mercy and love. As a result, I never for a single moment at any time felt abandoned by Him, and I was more sure than ever before of His will to heal.

Nevertheless, there was so much I wanted to do in Christ's service which was now impossible that at times I felt almost overwhelmed by frustration. During one such time I was reading Scripture, and Elisha's words to Elijah leaped from the page: "I pray thee, let a double portion of thy spirit be upon me" (II Kings 2:9).

Closing my Bible, I pondered these words, puzzled why they should seem meaningful, since within the context of the passage in which they occurred there was certainly no possible personal application. Still wondering, I re-opened the Bible at random, and my eyes fell upon the words, "They shall possess the double: everlasting joy shall be unto them" (Isa. 61:7).

Suddenly a great light shone: Impressed upon my heart was the conviction that the Lord rewards those who are afflicted, by a double portion of His Spirit. This, then, was the secret of the supernatural strength and grace which were mine, making the impossible possible. "I declare that I will render double unto thee" (Zech. 9:12). He has—and my gratitude, as my joy, is everlasting.

Through it all—the long hours spent in bed lying perfectly flat, unable to read because holding even a paperback book caused painful strain on the back; the months that ran into years during which I could be up only four hours at a time—I was to learn much by the teaching of the Spirit, much of prayer, and what it meant to be alone with God. And I was to learn that whatever *He* wanted me to do, He would make possible, and that which I thought I should be doing was often not at all necessary. That I have been able to continue to work and have never had to cancel a mission since that first hospitalization has been the continuing and marvelous evidence of the power of the Holy Spirit.

I was to learn what it was to be stripped of pride—so often, between connecting planes, I would be forced to lie down in airport waiting rooms, and on many occasions, on the floor of the airport's ladies' lounge.

I was to learn patience—and this in itself was a minor miracle, for by temperament I am impatient, hard-driving, hard-working, and filled with energy.

I was to learn a new compassion for all who suffer, for one who has not himself suffered cannot possibly fully comprehend it.

I was to learn experientially the validity of what I have so long taught: that when one is healed in spirit, the healing of the body is no longer of primary importance. Thus when people would say accusingly, "Why don't you ever speak of your back?" I could honestly reply, "Why should I? It's not that important."

Many have asked me how I became personally involved with the healing ministry. Let me begin by saying that probably no one is more surprised than I at the life I find myself leading. It has been a perfect illustration of what our Lord meant when He said, "Ye have not chosen me, but I have chosen you" (John 15:16). That He has seen fit to choose me to work in His ministry is just another example of the unlikely people He selects to work in His name.

God has given us free will to accept or reject Him, but although He has given us perfect freedom in His service, a curious paradox asserts itself: He draws us to Himself not by force, but nonetheless inexorably by love. This is precisely what happened to me.

As both my parents were atheists, I received no religious training and spent most of my life as an unbeliever, never bothering to find out what it was I didn't believe in. I was married in New York in a Park Avenue church because it was the socially acceptable thing to do, but from that day on it was to be many a year before my husband or I again saw the inside of a church. I had a wonderful husband, a graduate of the United States Naval Academy, who was later to become an executive of Gulf Oil Corporation. We had two beautiful children, and I became a successful free-lance magazine writer. Who needed or wanted God? Only the poor, the suffering, the weak, and we weren't any of these. And then I inadvertently attended a healing service. As a result of what seemed to be a purely haphazard accident, my life was to be forever changed.

To be sure, my first book had ended not as the exposé I had originally intended but as the story of my journey into faith. Nevertheless, I was a professional writer and this was just a book. True enough, I now believed in God, but at that time I certainly had no intention of devoting my entire life to Him. I was living a full and satisfying life, doing what I wanted to do and having fun doing it.

During the fall of 1956, when my first book was published, I was invited to speak at the International Order of St. Luke Conference, a religious conference in Philadelphia, which was attended by numerous clergymen. I received many requests to speak on the healing ministry and began to accept them. As my children were young and at home, I refused to leave them overnight, and wherever I went I managed to fly home the same day on which I spoke. There was one exception to this: I received and accepted an invitation to lead a three-day mission at an Episcopal church in a far-distant state.

At that time I had no idea what a "mission" was; all I knew was that I was to give three addresses on successive nights. When I arrived I was informed that each evening address was to be followed by a healing service at which I was to administer the laying on of hands with the participating clergy. I demurred strongly, never before having laid on hands or prayed for the sick. However, my protests were in vain, and in fear and trembling, I did what I was told.

The rector of the church was a firm believer in the healing ministry, but his new assistant did not share his sentiments. The young priest made abundantly clear his disapproval of both the ministry of healing and of me, a woman, performing a sacramental rite.

At the end of the second healing service the rector knelt in moving humility to receive the laying on of hands from me. Under the circumstances, the assistant rector could hardly fail to follow suit. As I laid hands on him, there was a loud crack, almost like a bomb exploding. I jumped, having no idea what had happened. Fifteen minutes later the mystery was solved: The crack had been the sound of a long-dislocated bone in the young man's body snapping back into place. It need hardly be added that the young assistant became at that moment one of the great champions of the healing ministry, and from that time on, I became increasingly involved in the ministry.

As I realized what was happening to my life, I fought, I kicked, I ran; but surely and relentlessly God pursued me. He caught and held me fast in the net of His love. Holding me there enmeshed, He transformed my life by His touch. He drove me to my knees not by force but by love. And by His love He has kept me there, no longer struggling, but now in complete happiness and joy.

I was to learn over the years that it is by love that God works. Love is His power to convert and change lives, His power to heal and to mend all brokenness. His love enables us to say, "I will not be offended in Him" (Matt. 26:33) no matter what happens, and His love calls us to obedience and makes it our joy to obey, no matter how rough the road or difficult the way.

I was to learn, as I had never even remotely conceived before, the fullness of the truth that God's grace is indeed sufficient, and that His strength is made perfect in weakness.

I was to learn that His grace and His strength never fail, and that with Him all things are indeed possible. And I was to have reaffirmed for all time the greatest of all His promises: "Lo, I am with you always, even unto the end of the world" (Matt. 28:20).

Chapter 2

Touch and Go: Conviction Confirmed

I REMEMBER WELL a woman in the terminal stage of cancer who flew to a healing service at Calvary accompanied by her nurse. I had agreed to speak with her for a few minutes before the service, and as she walked into the room the light of Christ emanated from her entire being. Her body was feeble and wracked with cancer, but she was filled with the joy of the Lord.

As she told me something of her condition, I asked her if she was afraid to die.

"Oh, no," she replied. "Actually I long to be wholly with Christ. However, as life is a gift of God, I felt I must do all possible to preserve it, lest there is more He wants me to do here. This is why I felt I had to come to Pittsburgh to attend this particular healing service."

In these words I heard the true Christian answer, and I knew this woman to be whole in Christ, regardless of the state of her body—and whether she lived or died.

After years of counseling and observation as well as experiential knowledge it is my firm conviction that one cannot live a true Christian life without having a Christian philosophy of death. That is, one cannot fully live the life abundant our Lord came to bring us (John 10:10) until we are unafraid to die, until we realize that at this very moment you and I are living in the midst of eternal life.

Death for the believer is not nihilism; it is the fullness of life in Christ. The early Christians lived with spiritual power and met death with joy because they knew this truth. The average Christian today either refuses to think of death at all, or his entire life is diminished because it is colored by what amounts to a psychopathic fear of death. It has long seemed to me that the problem of the Christian should not be his fear of death, but rather the dilemma expressed by Saint Paul when he said, "For me to live is Christ, and to die is gain. I am in a strait betwixt the two" (Phil. 1: 21, 23). Yet whenever I have spoken of death as the final triumph for the Christian, and not the ultimate disaster, a number of people have invariably said to me, "You can talk this way now—but just wait until you are faced with death, and you'll be as frightened of it as I am."

For a long time I had no answer to this, but now I have, for on a Tuesday evening several years ago, on my way to lead a mission in another state, I was faced with death. I was scheduled to make a connecting flight to my ultimate destination, but the connecting plane experienced mechanical trouble, and at five o'clock, after waiting in the airport for four hours, word came that this plane could not be repaired, and the next flight out would be the next morning.

It was imperative that I reach my destination that night. After much inquiring I discovered that an air-taxi service operated between where I was and where I was going. The next such flight was scheduled to leave at seven o'clock, so after telephoning the pastor of the mission church to say my plane was scheduled to arrive at 7:45, I took up my vigil at the air-taxi counter.

At last seven o'clock came, and I heard the welcome words, "Here comes the pilot now. As you're the only passenger, he'll take you in the two-seater."

I looked up, and could see no one coming except a middle-aged man in blue jeans and a torn sweater. This, it turned out, was the pilot.

He took my bags and led me to a tiny plane. There was no ramp, no steps, and when I asked, "How do you get in?" he replied, "You climb up on the wing and crawl in."

It had started to rain—a slight drizzle—and I shuddered to think of the state of my pale beige fur coat after crawling along the dirty, wet wing. But I clambered aboard, grateful for any transportation, and sat in the seat next to the pilot. The cabin was pitch-black except for the dim glow of the instrument panel in front of us.

About ten minutes after take-off, we ran into a severe storm. There was a deluge of rain, and great flashes of lightning seemed to split the sky in two. The small plane hurtled about like a piece of paper in a hurricane.

Time went on and on. It seemed to me that surely more than the forty-five-minute flight time had elapsed, but I could not see my watch in the darkness. It got colder and colder inside the plane, until my teeth were actually chattering. The pilot spoke briefly into the radio mouthpiece, but I was unable to hear what he said above the ear-splitting noise of the engine. He then took out of his pocket what appeared to be a map, and asked me to hold a flashlight while he studied it.

The plane took a sudden plunge, and just as suddenly, I knew that something was badly wrong. I yelled at the top of my lungs to be heard above the engine: "Is something wrong?" By a scarcely perceptible shrug of his shoulders, I knew that the pilot had heard my question—and I also knew that he would not answer for fear of frightening me.

As the lightning and the plunging of the plane grew worse, I yelled again, "Please, I'm not afraid"—and the wonder of it was, I was telling the truth—"but I want to know. We *are* in trouble, aren't we?"

This time the pilot turned toward me and nodded. Then he did a kind and lovely thing: He reached out with his right hand and took my left, and squeezed it. By this compassionate gesture, I knew in just what serious trouble we were.

"I'm going to try to land," he said. "We can't possibly make it any further."

I could feel the plane descend. Rushing down in the blackness of the night, a small light seemed to leap forward to meet us. It was a light from a house. Far off in the distance to our right appeared the runway we were trying to make.

The plane ascended again, and the pilot said, "I'll have to make another try for it."

It was then that I realized that the radio was out. We had no communication with the airport, and visibility was zero. There was no radar to assist us, and at this point I realized that our chances of landing safely were virtually nil. I knew that I faced death.

Thoughts of my children flashed through my mind, and I wondered who would tell them. Then I prayed for the pilot, made a quick act of contrition, and with my hand in the hand of Christ—so close was He—I suddenly felt the greatest joy I have ever experienced. Wherever I was going, it was not into the unknown. Crystal clear I heard the words: "Today shalt thou be with me in paradise" (Luke 23:43).

What more does a Christian really need to know? Having long prayed that I might burn out and not rust out in

His service, I now felt an overwhelming gratitude for answered prayer.

"Into Thy hands, O God, I commend our spirits—that of the pilot and mine," I said aloud. And then, my voice drowned out by the roar of the engine, I sang lustily the Nunc Dimittis: "Lord, now lettest thou thy servant depart in peace, according to thy word. For mine eyes have seen thy salvation, which thou hast prepared before the face of all people; To be a light to lighten the Gentiles, and to be the glory of thy people Israel" (Luke 2:29–32). As I sang "Glory be to the Father and to the Son and to the Holy Ghost," I felt a tremendous jarring. My back seemed broken and my body strained so hard against the seat belt it seemed it must be cut in two. Then I felt the eerie sensation of standing on my head. Opening my eyes, I saw that we were nose-down in a field about two hundred yards from the runway. The pilot grabbed me, dragged me out of the plane, and told me to run in case of fire. As we ran over the rough field, stumbling and almost falling, three men ran out from the tiny airport building to meet us. "My God!" one cried, "We thought you'd gone down for sure!"

The pilot looked at me, took both my hands in his, and replied, "We ran into a bit of a storm, and had a little navigation trouble. With the radio out, I was flying completely blind."

I looked now at my watch. It was just after ten-thirty. We had been up in the air for over three and one-half hours.

By now storm warnings were out, and all planes were grounded. One of the men at the airport offered to take me in his car to my destination, a two-hour drive away. Before leaving, I called the pastor, who had been waiting for me for three hours. At eight-thirty he had been told that there was no word from my plane, which was apparently lost. At nine they closed the airport, and the pastor and his wife sat just outside the shut door near a telephone booth in case I should call. They had been in prayer the entire time they were waiting and had planned to remain there until midnight. If by then they had heard nothing, they were prepared to call my bishop in Pittsburgh and ask him to notify the children.

Meanwhile, the pilot and I, who had been through this experience together, had become the closest of friends, although we did not even know one another's name. We threw our arms around each other before we separated, and his parting words were: "I'm so sorry about this. It was the closest call I've ever had." Then, as an afterthought, he added, "Hey—how come you weren't scared?"

All I could think of to say was, "Because by the grace of God I am a Christian."

"Me, too," he said.

As I walked out of the little building, I said to him, "Be careful—and God bless and keep you."

He replied, "God was awfully close tonight, wasn't He?" I just nodded and stepped into the waiting car.

Now in the telling of this story and my own reaction to what I believed was impending death, I do not mean to imply that I don't love life. I do—and so should all Christians. But I also believe that all Christians should look forward to death with the joy of Saint Paul, knowing as he did that death is only another dimension of eternal life, and that in death lies that perfect wholeness which alone can be found in the fullness of Christ.

The mission that I had so nearly missed was marvelously blessed. The people's hope, expectancy, and hunger for God were vividly apparent—and He honored those elements with an almost incredibly abundant outpouring of the Holy Spirit.

There were healings of every kind: of fear and anxiety and depression, of broken relationships, of grief, and of course there were numerous physical healings. These included the instantaneous disappearance of a large abdominal tumor, the restoration of vision to one long blind, and the disappearance of symptoms of advanced Parkinson's disease (the woman wrote me a letter several weeks later, the first letter she had been able to write in fifteen years because of the tremor of her hands).

The case of a woman healed of crippling arthritis was particularly interesting. She had come to me the first day of the mission, bent double, walking with great difficulty with the aid of two canes. She was a woman of great faith, and at the end of our talk, I said, "In the name of Jesus, walk." Her back straightened, she handed me her canes, arose from her chair, and walked three times around the room. At first her steps were hesitant, then firm and sure. She came to all of the services, where she offered thanksgiving and prayed for others. Like the woman during our Lord's earthly ministry, she was permanently loosed from her infirmity (Luke 13: 10–17).

Then there were multitudinous healings of ruptured discs and spinal ailments of various kinds. Curiously enough, these are a frequent occurrence at healing services ever since the original injury to my own spine. I have never before witnessed so many healings of spinal trouble as over the past six years.

The healing of a little girl of about eight, of a minor affliction—warts—was one of the healings for which I was most grateful.

In the opening address of the mission, I had told of inadvertently attending my first healing service years before, when a little boy was healed of his warts. (Actually this healing had not impressed me at the time, knowing as I did that warts spontaneously disappear.)

On the second evening of the mission the little girl whispered to her mother, "Mrs. Neal says that God cares about my warts and will take them away, so I'm going up to receive the laying on of hands." Up she trotted with the glorious faith of a little child, and God did indeed take away her warts. To me healings of this kind are as wonderful as the healing of any cancer. They demonstrate so beautifully that to God nothing that concerns His children is unimportant or unworthy of His healing love, and that He is beyond all doubt a personal God, who knows the number of hairs on each of our heads and is aware of each sparrow which falls to the ground (Matt. 10:29, 30).

When I learned of the healing of this child, I remembered a small boy in Pittsburgh for whom we have long prayed, but who has not as yet been physically healed. Tommy, deaf in one ear, is the son of an Episcopal priest of great faith in the healing Christ. He laid hands on his son regularly, for a long, long time, completely convinced that his hearing would be restored. "Finally," he says, "I realized that Tommy was not going to be physically healed—at least not right now. So I changed my prayer to: 'God, if he can't hear me, let him hear You.'" The prayer of this father was answered. Tommy is extraordinarily close to God, and who among us would dare to say that this child is not whole?

Twisting to get in and out of the plane, plus the extremely rough landing, had badly injured my back again, and the effects of the accident would be with me for years to come. But I was so overwhelmed by the power of God manifested during this mission that my own injury seemed completely insignificant. When the final service was over and the people had gone home, the participating clergy, as overjoyed and exhilarated as myself, were talking together in the sacristy as they devested. I slipped away unnoticed and knelt at the altar rail of the now darkened and empty church, thanking God for the awesome power of the Holy Spirit which had been so evident during the past three days. Offering Him once more my injured back to be used for His glory, I prayed with all my heart that if because of my pain I were to be a more open channel for His healing grace, He permit me to keep it.

I was to think often of this prayer in the months to come, as the power of the Spirit seemed greater than ever before. I was fully aware of that narrow line between a neurotic desire to suffer, which then makes us impervious to the healing power of the resurrected Christ, and offering to Him the suffering we have, at the same time praying that His perfect will for wholeness be fulfilled in us. In the end I was satisfied that I was on the right side of the line. Hating pain of itself, I was not rejoicing in my infirmity because I then had more to offer God. I could not embrace the pain as pain—but I could embrace it as the cross by which I could share in Christ's death, and thus inevitably in His Resurrection.

If for reasons I did not understand God was using this pain as I knew He was—perhaps to purge and cleanse that I might be an increasingly open channel; perhaps to protect me from spiritual pride in order that I might be a better instrument—then I would not only gladly endure, but "glory in my infirmity that the power of Christ might rest upon me" (II Cor. 12:9). For the reason for my being was that He might be glorified and manifested through me.

This is not to say that in the pain-filled years ahead I did not falter. I did. It is not to say that I was never discouraged or at times demoralized by pain. I was. It is merely to say that in His mercy I never felt forsaken.

Chapter 3

LEAVE THE METHOD TO GOD

SOME TIME AGO, a young minister telephoned me long distance to ask prayer for his ill wife. During the course of our conversation, he remarked, "If my wife is healed, she will make a powerful witness. God will *really* be glorified in my church. This is why I'm so certain that she *must* be healed."

As I heard these words, my heart sank. Time and time again I have heard this rationale for healing expressed, and almost invariably the individual who is to *"really glorify God"* through his healing witness fails to recover. Why should this be? Surely it appears a worthy motive to desire healing so the kingdom may be advanced. I have spent many hours pondering this question and the seeming paradox involved. Gradually I have come to conclude that it is not the avowed motive but the attitude behind it which is at fault.

In our knowledge of the healing Christ and our subsequent enthusiasm for the healing ministry, we are often led astray by the false assumption that God can be glorified only by a witness of physical healing. The truth is that some of the most effective Christian witnesses I know are those who are lying flat on their backs expectantly awaiting their healing by God's grace and at the same time are offering their suffering to be used for His glory. I have seen the light of Christ shine with blinding radiance in the eyes of those who are suffering in His name and for His sake.

Those who are enabled by grace (for no one can do it on his own) to suffer redemptively are far more whole than the individual who may enjoy perfect physical health yet is spiritually dead.

It is not difficult to glorify God when one receives physical healing. It is when one suffers yet never loses his faith in the healing Christ, when one offers his life to God, confident that in His own way and time He will bestow His gift of healing, that Christ can be glorified—sometimes even more effectively than if an instantaneous physical healing were to occur.

If my heart sank at the young minister's stated reason for his assurance that his wife would be healed by the power of God, it plunged at his next words: "Of course, Betty can be cured by simple surgery, but she will make a better witness if God heals her without medical intervention."

Entirely unwittingly this young clergyman, as so many others with this same attitude, was, in my opinion, guilty of the sin of presumption. As God does not tolerate a lack of humility, so He does not tolerate its twin, presumption. To tell God how He must heal, to demand that He heal in only one way, namely by the direct intervention of His Holy Spirit, is surely an act of presumptive arrogance on our part.

All knowledge is of God, given and revealed to men by Him—and medicine is part of this knowledge. To reject it is to reject a gift of God. The purpose of the healing ministry is not to eradicate medicine, but to seek that cooperation of medicine and religion which will best assure the total wholeness of the individual.

Most certainly we pray for healing, but the means must be left to God. Sometimes He uses physicians, sometimes He heals without. Sometimes He uses surgeons, sometimes He Himself is the surgeon. I think particularly of a woman with a breast tumor. The morning following healing prayer the tumor had not only disappeared, but a thin, white scar, perfectly healed, was clearly visible. However, in the prayer that had been offered for this woman, we did not presume to tell God how to heal her. She had been scheduled for surgery within the week, and we had offered thanksgiving that God had revealed to man the means of skillful surgery, and that it was available to those who needed it. We prayed for the guidance of the surgeon, asking that the Great Physician heal according to His will. In this case, as in many, it was His will to heal by the direct intervention of the Holy Spirit.

Properly practiced, the healing ministry works in cooperation with the medical profession; it never seeks to supplant it. As physicians learn that we do not advocate that the sick stop their medication or discard their crutches, the original skepticism and hostility toward this ministry by the medical profession is being replaced by the endorsement of a growing number of doctors. Many of these who have seen medically inexplicable healings in their practice are now willing to attribute such healings to the power of God released by prayer.

In those instances where God chooses to heal through physicians, healing prayer gives strength and courage to the patient, and almost invariably he makes an unusually rapid recovery. A typical example is the case of a woman who recently underwent a mastectomy. Apprehensive and fearful, she attended a healing service the evening before she entered the hospital. As a result, she went to surgery unafraid and in great peace. She made an extraordinarily rapid recovery, suffering virtually no pain whatsoever and refusing sedation. This kind of rapid and uneventful recovery of the dedicated Christian has been remarked by many physicians, including Dr. Graham Clark, eye surgeon at Columbia Presbyterian Medical Center in New York.

Healing prayer results in a divine quickening of the entire healing process—a quickening which can be rather mundanely likened to the baking of a potato in a microwave oven, which takes just a few minutes, rather than in an ordinary oven, which takes an hour. And not only does the cooperation of medicine and religion result in more rapid healing, but in more complete healing. Here the spirit as well as the body is involved, and thus the wholeness of the individual is assured—that wholeness of the entire nature of man, which comprises body, mind, and spirit.

Misconceptions of the healing ministry are many and varied. Not long ago, for example, I received a letter from a woman, obviously distraught, asking prayer for her critically ill child. The woman knew nothing of the healing ministry, but someone had given her my name, and she had written in sheer desperation. She ended her letter by saying, "A friend told me to take my daughter to healing services, or at least for me to go on her behalf as intercessor. This I refuse to do, as I don't believe in *forcing* God."

In my reply I explained that the healing ministry is in no way an attempt to coerce an unwilling God into healing. Instead, it is an attempt to permit His perfect will for wholeness to be fulfilled in us. He proffers us His healing because of His boundless mercy and love—not in reluctant response to any efforts of ours to "force" Him to heal. God cannot be forced. He does not coerce us, nor will He be coerced by us. He heals out of pure compassion. This was one of our Lord's great revelations concerning the nature of God. Throughout His earthly ministry Jesus healed all who came to Him, thus revealing for all time the will of God in respect to disease and brokenness of every kind.

In the case of this medically incurable child, whose mother was to learn what the healing ministry really meant, God healed by the direct intervention of His Spirit.

Over the centuries countless lives have been lost because people have not believed or sought the healing power of the risen Christ. Conversely, many needlessly die today, because they eschew God's revealed knowledge, and insist that they be healed in a manner according to their wills, and not His.

In the recent past, an out-of-state couple flew to Pittsburgh to attend a healing service at Calvary. The woman had a large abdominal tumor, the man a double hernia. In the conference I had with them just prior to the service they told me that they had come to be made whole in Christ. This was a proper motive, and indeed the reason for the Calvary services. They had come, they assured me, filled with expectant faith. This was good, for expectancy is one of the laws of healing. Yet neither of them had consulted a physician since the original diagnosis had been made.

I explained to them that the healing ministry was not a substitute for medicine, that a healing service is not the equivalent of a visit to a doctor's office. I told them there should be close cooperation between medicine and the healing ministry. Nevertheless, frequently when physicians have given up all hope for a patient's recovery, the patient is healed by the power of God.

This couple had refused to return to their physician because, they said, their faith in God to heal made medical treatment unnecessary. This may have proved true in their case; it has been so in many others, but only when the patient leaves the method of healing in God's hands. The attitude of this couple disturbed me, for they were in a very real sense delivering an ultimatum to God: "He is going to heal us here and now—or else."

This is where the presumption comes in, that sin of the spirit which so often impedes the healing power of God. It is not that He ever intentionally withholds His healing, but any sin separates us from God, creating a divisive chasm across which His power cannot flow. It is not He who will not heal, but we who cannot receive that grace He stands always so ready to pour upon us.

It is a basic tenet of the faith that God works through men; and thus He works through doctors, even if the physician is not a Christian. God is the God of both atheist and believer. He exists whether or not we acknowledge Him, and not one of us on this earth could draw a single breath were it not for the Holy Spirit.

The couple to whom I attempted to explain all this had mixed reactions. The man understood what I was saying. The woman was angry—so angry that at the service she did not come up for the laying on of hands with prayer. Her husband did; he came not for himself, but for his wife, that she might understand what I had attempted to tell her.

This story had a happy and, it seems to me, extremely significant ending. The husband was himself completely healed by God, and his prayers for his wife were answered. She wrote me an apology for her attitude, telling me that she had reconsidered and gone to her physician. He had recommended surgery, and she wrote me several weeks after her operation. The tumor was benign, and her recovery was remarkably rapid. She stated in her letter: "I see now what you meant. I prayed for my surgeon and for my healing, and God healed me as surely through surgery as by the direct intervention of the Holy Spirit.

The hand of the Great Physician was on my surgeon's hand, and Jesus Himself stood with us in the operating room. I thank God for my doctors and for His healing grace made manifest in me."

A Pittsburgh woman attending the Calvary services offers a good example of one who committed an entire situation to God to do with according to His will. Her husband, a man in his forties, suffered from cataracts. He was under the care of an ophthalmologist who was awaiting the proper time to operate—which, the physician cautioned, would not be for a considerable length of time. Cataracts must reach a certain degree of "ripeness" before they are operable, and this ripeness occurs only when the patient is virtually blind. The waiting process is tedious and nerve-racking.

In addition to his frightening physical condition, this man was deeply worried about his work. He was a salesman on the road all week, necessarily driving his car wherever he went. As well as his wife, he had young children to support, and with encroaching blindness his job was in serious jeopardy. He was as concerned and anxious over the almost inevitable loss of his job as he was over the condition of his eyes.

The wife came to Calvary to intercede and receive the laying on of hands for her husband. Her first prayers were for the immediate healing of his eyes—and then suddenly a new thought came to her, surely inspired by the Holy Spirit. She changed her prayers to this effect: "Lord, I know that it is Your holy will that Bob be healed, and I know that You *will* heal him. But the *method* of Your healing I leave in Your hands. I pray therefore that Bob be either quickly healed—or that the cataracts will rapidly worsen to the point that the surgeon can operate. Whatever is Your will, I thank You for this healing."

The following Friday night when Bob came home for the weekend, he walked in the front door and said to his

wife, "Sit down, honey, I have to tell you something."
They sat down together on the sofa. As he put his arm
around her, he said, "Now pull yourself together. I know
that you've been praying for my healing, but God's
answer is 'No.'" Bob paused for a moment and then
delivered his blow: "I'm almost totally blind. It happened all of a sudden this afternoon, and I had to leave
the car in Cleveland and fly home."

To Bob's utter amazement, his wife cried out ecstatically, "Thank God! My prayers were answered!"

At her husband's look of bewilderment, she explained.
"Don't you understand? Now you can be operated on
during your vacation, and you'll be as good as new
when it's time to go back to work!"

That is precisely what happened. She drove her husband to the doctor next morning. The eye surgeon ex-
amined Bob, and surgery was scheduled for the following
Tuesday morning. The operation was totally successful.

This is not to say that we are not confident that it is
God's primary will that we be healed—but the timing
and the method of the healing must be left to Him. This
does not mean that we should not expect instantaneous
healing. We should, for we should always expect the
most, just so long as we do not attempt to dictate to God,
and by our presumption thwart the working of the Holy
Spirit.

God chose His own way to heal Bob. For reasons we do
not know, He has chosen to heal others with the same
affliction without surgery. Dr. C. B. King, an ophthalmologist in Canton, Ohio, reports, for example, that a
patient came to him from another town for an eye examination. Dr. King found his eyes almost perfect. This man
then told the physician that several years before, he had
suffered cataracts in both eyes. Following the custom-
ary procedure, his ophthalmologist was awaiting the
proper time for surgery. Meanwhile, as the patient's vision

worsened, his driver's license was revoked. This man then began attending healing services, praying for healing in God's own way. He was completely healed by the power of God without surgery. Dr. King issued him a medical certificate, and the man's driver's license was subsequently reinstated.

To demand that God heal in a particular way, according to our own desire, is to attempt to make of Him a celestial lackey. We must ask Him for the fulfillment of His holy will in us. We must place our confidence in Him, knowing that He never makes a mistake; that whatever way He choses to heal is the best way for us under our circumstances and is in accordance with His plan for us.

We go to Him in prayer; we come to His healing church in order to be made whole in Him. At the same time, we obey the admonishment to "honor the physician with the honor due him," for "He gave skill to men that He might be glorified in His marvelous works. There is a time when success lies in the hands of physicians, for they, too, will pray to the Lord" (Ecclus. 38:1, 6, 13 R.S.V.).

We should not, therefore, eschew the God-given knowledge of men, but neither should we ever forget the vital necessity of prayer so that we may be not only physically healed but made spiritually whole. It is Christ who integrates our total personality, and through Him we receive healing on a far deeper level than medicine alone can provide.

Chapter 4

"ALL SORTS AND CONDITIONS OF MEN"

NOT LONG AGO a self-avowed atheist categorically stated: "One has to be of a certain temperament, a particular emotional make-up, if one is to accept the Christian faith."

This statement is totally erroneous. First, Christ died for all men, and the gospel is equally applicable to everyone. Second, a mere glance at the history of the faith and some of its great leaders makes clear the extraordinarily wide diversity of temperament among Christians throughout the ages.

We see in Saint Peter, for example, a wavering, rather unstable personality; in Saint Paul, an unequivocating and authoritarian theologian. Later, we see the simple poet, Christ-like Saint Francis; the intellectual and self-willed Saint Augustine; the brilliant philosopher and theologian, Saint Thomas Aquinas; the illiterate French peasant, the Curé d'Ars, who could not pass his theological examinations and for years was refused permission by the church to hear confessions, but who became one of the church's great priests to whom thousands flocked from all over France, including some of the great dignitaries of the church.

From the beginning of Christianity there have always been disciples of markedly different temperaments and talents, and so it is today. There is no one "Christian temperament," and this is particularly evident in the healing ministry, where we see all denominations commingle. There is room in the faith for all backgrounds and emotional make-ups, from the Pentecostals to the most conservative Eastern Orthodox churches, from factory workers to business executives, from poets to scientists. The one great bond is love, by which the Spirit of God binds one to another.

We are all one in Christ, but fortunately we are not one in our talents or intellects or emotional responses. Christianity is for all people for all time. Our Lord was not crucified for "specialists," and each and every Christian has something peculiarly his own to bring to Christ and His body.

A woman with several small children once said to me, "I feel swamped in a bog of trivia. I'm not doing anything worthwhile for Christ—just washing clothes and getting meals."

I reminded her of Brother Lawrence (*The Practice of the Presence of God*) and of how, amidst his pots and pans, he glorified God. Nothing, no matter what it may be, is "trivial" if it is done for the glory of God.

During His earthly ministry of healing, our Lord ministered to people of every conceivable background. He met each one's need by the appropriate method. Although the sacramental healing rite of the laying on of hands is offered in obedience to our Lord's command, "They shall lay hands on the sick and they shall recover" (Mark 16:18), and although He himself used this method (Luke 4:40, 41), He was not bound by it; He healed in a number of different ways, as the situation and the personality warranted.

He healed frequently by touch, as in the case of the widow of Nain's son (Luke 7:11–15); by word, as with the centurion's servant (Luke 8:8). He healed by intercession (the Syrophoenician woman's daughter, Matt. 15:21–28); by anointing (the blind man, John 9:6). He healed through the forgiveness of sins, as in the case of the palsied man (Mark 2:3–12), and by exorcism, as with the dumb demoniac (Matt. 9:32, 33).

And so it is today: Particular illnesses, particular temperaments, may respond to different methods. Thus when people ask, "Must one receive the sacramental healing rites to be healed?" the answer is obviously "No."

Thousands have been healed by prayer alone, by petition and intercession. Many have been healed by simply reading about the power of God to heal, or by watching religious television programs, or by listening to radio evangelists. However, times without number, when we lay on hands in response to our Lord's specific command, people who have hitherto remained unhealed receive healing.

It is often and truly said that Christ commissioned His church to preach, to teach, and to heal. However, in respect to specific ministries of the church, I would alter these three imperatives to: "Preach the gospel, heal the sick, and do this in remembrance of Me." This is what our Lord said, and in this order. These words indicate to me three separate and distinct ministries.

Jesus did not say, "Preach the gospel, and as a result, the sick will be healed." While this sometimes happens, what He actually said was, "Preach the gospel *and* heal the sick" (Luke 9:2).

While I have often said that the sacrament of holy communion is the greatest of all healing services, and while many have indeed been healed through this sacrament, still one lays on hands out of obedience. The many members of religious communities who have been healed through the laying on of hands offer ample evidence that He meant what He said. These religious receive holy communion every day of their lives; they are recipients of remarkably powerful intercessory prayer when in need; yet many monastics have not been physically healed until they receive the specific healing rites.

At the other end of the spectrum are the non-sacramentalists who have been led to receive the sacramental rites and have received a miracle. I think in this regard of a woman almost totally incapacitated by a progressive crippling disease. Her husband is a minister in a non-liturgical church, and both to him and his wife any sacramental approach was anathema.

The sick woman had been prayed for for many months, apparently to no avail. It was during a healing mission that her husband sought me out. As his church is noted for its supposedly undeviating adherence to Scripture, I spoke to him of the scriptural authority for the laying on of hands; but his prejudice against the sacramental was too deeply ingrained to be quickly eradicated. However, he capitulated to the extent of taking one of my books home to his wife.

It was during the week following, which she had spent in studying the book, that she awoke suddenly in the middle of the night with the conviction that if she could receive the sacramental healing rite she would be healed. She awakened her husband and asked him to lay on hands.

He told me later, "I was in a state akin to panic. I didn't like the sacramental approach, and of course I had never in my life used it or that kind of healing prayer. But I saw how much it meant to her, so I went ahead."

As a result, his wife dramatically improved. The full use of her arms and hands has been restored, and she is able to take long walks, aided only by a cane, which she is certain she will soon be able to discard. She receives the laying on of hands regularly from her husband, who is no longer reluctant but eager to minister to her —and to his people—in this way. In her case, as in so many, the laying on of hands served as her point of contact with the healing Christ.

As there is also scriptural authority for unction (anointing with oil) for healing (James 5:14), many ask about the respective uses of these two rites. Although some churches use one or the other or both, personal observation leads me to believe that the laying on of hands is best used in public healing services, and unction reserved for private use in the sickroom. There are several reasons for this; among them is the fact that many who attend healing services come as intecessors, receiving the laying on of hands with special intention for another. This cannot be properly done with unction, which must be administered directly to the individual in need.

We can't fence God in, nor can we pigeonhole Jesus. God is not the private property of any one type of person or of any one branch of the church. The Holy Spirit works with power in evangelistic meetings and liturgical church services alike. The healing Christ will not be confined, and the ministry of healing is the great catalyst —not a *leveler*, but a *raiser*—where believing Christians are uniquely united by their faith in the healing Christ.

As the healing power of God is not restricted to any one church or method, neither is His response to prayer limited to any one form of supplication. This was beautifully illustrated during a recent mission. An extremely ill Episcopal priest was in attendance. After one of the services, he sent word that he wanted to see me. As we talked, it was clear that he was a strict Anglo-Catholic, and I realized that it was difficult for him to come to me, a woman, for help. I also realized how difficult it would be for him to receive a sacramental rite from a lay woman.

When it came time for the laying on of hands and healing prayer, I sensed intuitively that this very Catholic, older priest would feel more comfortable if some of his fellow-clergy were to participate. I asked him if he would like me to go back into the church and gather together any priests I could find. He nodded, so I did just this, managing to locate four.

We all laid hands on the sick man together, while I prayed the healing prayer. But it was not I who prayed, it was the Holy Spirit, Who knew far better than I how best to meet this man's need. I suddenly found myself on my knees and heard myself saying some of the great liturgical prayers that I didn't even realize I knew from memory. These were prayers which this priest loved and understood, and through them God worked to bless and heal.

The other priests joined with me as the prayers were concluded with the Sanctus from the Episcopal service of Holy Communion. Tears of peace and joy streamed down the sick man's face.

Immediately following this episode, a Pentecostal came to talk with me about his problem. Obviously his prayer-need could not be met with liturgical prayers from the Episcopal Book of Common Prayer. For him, the Holy Spirit prayed in me in an entirely different way, this time pleading the Blood of Jesus. This prayer the supplicant understood, and was blessed by God through it.

God meets the need wherever it is, and the Holy Spirit intercedes according to His will (Rom. 8:27). Thus the prayer-requirement, whatever the background or temperament of the supplicant, is met.

The diversity of temperament among all Christians emphasizes the dual nature of each believer: The Christian knows that joy which no man can take from him and at the same time carries within himself a broken heart. Our hearts break because we know that by our sins we continue to break the heart of God. They break for the world, and for all those who suffer. Yet as we seek to fulfill the law of Christ by bearing one another's burdens (Gal. 6:2), we are simultaneously filled with a curious joy. It is as if our hearts, broken as they are by the world's suffering, nonetheless serve as receptacles for the joy we have in Christ—for we know that in Him all suffering is overcome.

In the healing ministry we speak continually of claiming the promises of Jesus. These promises do not apply to only one kind of person; they are for all believers. "Ask, and it shall be given you" (Matt. 7:7), our Lord said; "And all things, whatsoever ye shall ask in prayer, believing, ye shall receive" (Matt. 21:22).

There is a condition implicit in these and all His promises; namely, that we must ask according to His will. Everything we ask of God must be founded on His basic premise and fundamental promise: "If ye abide in me, and my words abide in you, ye shall ask what ye will, and it shall be done unto you" (John 15:7).

So no matter what we ask of Him, it is a primary condition that we abide in God and His words abide in us. Only then can we say with the confidence of Jeremiah, "Heal me, O Lord, and I shall be healed; save me, and I shall be saved" (Jer. 17:14).

"If thou canst believe, all things are possible to him that believeth" (Mark 9:23). We pray for that sort of dynamic faith that enables us to *really* believe that all things are possible with God. But as we pray, we must watch our motivation: We must determine whether we desire the gift of faith merely that we may receive what we think we want, or whether we desire it so that we may believe in Him Whom we ask.

I remember well a man suffering a veritable hell of

pain, who could not get his mind off the pain long enough to want in his heart anything but relief from his agony. His nurse, an unbeliever, looked askance when I spoke to him of the love of God, of how Jesus suffered for him, of how Christ looked upon him now with infinite compassion, suffering for and with him.

As I spoke, this man understood for just a fleeting second something of God's love; and for just a moment he wanted God Himself—the experiential knowledge that God did indeed abide in him. That moment was enough, and the pain left him.

To claim the promises of Jesus means to stand firm in our conviction that God does not lie, and that if we ask according to His will, it shall be given us. And we can know, with a knowledge of the spirit given by the Spirit, that "Eye hath not seen nor ear heard, neither have entered into the heart of man, the things which God hath prepared for them that love him" (I Cor. 2:9).

When we dare to claim His promises, marvelous things happen—but if they are to happen, we must be in His will. This is what He means when He says, "Verily I say unto you, whatsoever ye shall ask the Father in my name, He will give it to you" (John 16:23). To ask in His name is to request according to the will of God: otherwise we dare not ask. To know His will means to desist from asking, and to remain silent so that we may hear. It means to empty ourselves of self, so that we may be filled with His Holy Spirit. It means to stop champing at the bit of our own desires and learn to wait patiently, quietly, and confidently, until in peace He leads us to that door He wants us to walk through, the door that leads us to the next portion of the plan He has for the lives of each one of us. This is all we need to do, but of all things it is the most difficult, so anxious are we to manage and manipulate our own lives, making our own important decisions apart from God.

Here the line is close between a complete and vacant

passivity where we do nothing but coast aimlessly along, and a creative, active response in which we do indeed take action—but by God's, not our own, volition. For it is God and not ourselves in whom we live and move and have our being (Acts 17:28).

The promises He made were to His first disciples, who knew and loved Him well. Thus they were made to us, regardless of our church affiliation, our color, our background, or our temperament. He says to us as He said to those who followed Him two thousand years ago: "I am come a light into the world, that whosoever believeth on me, should not abide in darkness" (John 12: 47); "If any man serve me, let him follow me" (John 12:26).

As we are inheritors of the kingdom, but must claim it if we are to possess it, so, if we would claim His promises, must we believe in our heart His words when He says, "I am the way, the truth, and the life" (John 14:6). For without Him, we cannot find the way; we cannot know the truth; and we have no life.

Chapter 5

DELAYED HEALINGS

INSTANTANEOUS HEALINGS have increased greatly over the past few years, due most probably to the slowly but surely growing faith of the church. Nevertheless the majority of healings today are gradual.

This is in contradistinction to our Lord's earthly healing ministry, where all the healings recorded in Scripture were instantaneous; the only exception is the case of the blind man at Bethsaida (Mark 8:22–25).

Our Lord laid hands on him, and then asked if he could see. The man said, "I see men as trees, walking." Jesus immediately laid His hands again upon the man's eyes. When He removed them this time, the once-blind man was completely healed. He was now "restored and saw every man clearly."

During a recent mission I was privileged to witness a healing which was startling in its similarity to this gospel account. There was a young woman who worked nights and thus was unable to attend the mission's evening healing services. She asked, therefore, if she might bring her long-blind mother to the church next day to receive the laying on of hands with prayer. I agreed, and we arranged to meet in the rector's study after the morning session in the church. (In cases like this it is impossible to minister to one individual in the church during the day. The entire congregation seems possessed of a sixth sense, and everyone present at the daytime sessions wants to come up for the laying on of hands. This results in two healing services a day, which is an impossible situation when there are hundreds on whom to lay hands.)

Immediately after the morning service, I met with the daughter and her mother as planned. After the blind woman had received the healing rite, she said, "I can see light." Then she seemed to focus her eyes on the cross around my neck, and said in a hushed tone, "I see a great concentration of light in the form of a cross."

The daughter, very excited, asked, "Mother, can you see what color dress Mrs. Neal is wearing?"

The older woman shook her head. "It is pale," she said, "but I can't tell the color."

The account of the blind man in Scripture flashed through my mind. Following the example of Jesus, I quickly laid my hands again upon the woman's eyes, and I prayed. When I had finished, she looked straight at me. Tears of joy streamed down her face as she said in an awe-struck voice, "Now I can really see you, Mrs. Neal. You have on a white dress and a silver cross is around your neck." Her vision was completely restored.

This healing was delayed only a few moments. Why is it that most healings are considerably more gradual? Sometimes the reason is obvious. There may be blocks within the individual, spiritual sins such as resentment or hostility that impede the inflow of God's healing power. When such factors do not appear to exist, we must suppose that the delay in healing is due to a weakness of faith in the church as a whole. This was the belief and the explanation of the ancient church when healings failed to occur. Then there is the self-evident fact that none of us is Jesus Christ, and hence we are not the completely open channels for healing that He was. Finally, I am not convinced that there is not divine purpose in many delayed healings.

I think often of some of the instant and extremely dramatic healings I have witnessed: the man long paralyzed who walked; the woman instantly healed of skin cancer; the man long deaf whose ears were opened. All failed to return to give thanks, and all of them promptly forgot or ignored the source of all healing. The spirits of these individuals were left untouched, and thus they were not healed in the way that matters most. They were not made whole, and it is wholeness we seek in the healing ministry. We consider the ten lepers, only one of whom returned to give thanks for his healing. It was to this one alone that our Lord said, "Thy faith hath made thee whole" (Luke 17:11–19).

While it is true that in many cases the healing of the spirit—the closer union with God, which is the primary purpose of the ministry of healing—*follows* a physical healing, in most cases the healing of the spirit comes first.

A typical example is the case of a woman suffering from a large ovarian tumor who attended a healing mission about a year ago. When she and I had a brief conference during the mission, I found her seething with jealousy, bitterness, and resentment. I explained to her that unless she was liberated from these destructive emotions, her chances of physical healing were slight indeed. Thus we made the burden of our prayer not the disappearance of her tumor by the intervention of the Holy Spirit, but the taking by Him of her spiritual sins which were hindering the inflow of His grace in her life. A wonderful thing happened to this woman, as it has to so many others. She told me later that after the healing prayer that evening at the service, the power of God came down upon her so mightily that it went through her body like an electric current and continued to do so throughout the night. A letter from her not long ago related that since the last night of the mission she had lost all her resentment, that she has been steadily growing in the knowledge and love of God; and since that time, her tumor has shrunk slowly but surely, until a recent medical examination proved it to be nonexistent.

Roots and pieces of what had been the growth were gradually eliminated by her system over a period of seven or eight months. All during these months this woman had engaged in a spiritual struggle. Because she had been highly expectant of instant healing, regardless of what I had said about the necessity of being rid of her own spiritual impediments, the fact that the power of God had flowed so strongly through her body that night of the mission had led her to think I had been mistaken—that she was indeed going to receive the instantaneous healing she sought. She reasoned that she would take care of the hatreds and resentments with which she was filled *after* her physical healing. But it didn't work that way. God's power going through her body was the seal of His promise that she would be healed when she met the requirements. I can only believe that it was God's purpose that her physical healing be delayed, so that when it came, she would be in every way whole.

In my own case, while I have been quickly healed of many ailments, the healing of my back has been torturously slow—but I believe that not one second of suffering has been wasted. This suffering was not the primary will of God, nor did He send it—of this I am certain. But I am equally certain that He has used my suffering for His glory and for His own holy purpose.

While we await the completion of a gradual healing, no suffering need ever be fruitless or unavailing. For while it is true that we believe that disease is not of the kingdom of God, we also know that when it is offered to Him it becomes His, and thus He sanctifies both it and the sufferer. Further, in a way we cannot pretend to understand but neither can we doubt, He will use our suffering on behalf of others if we will only ask Him. This is a powerful faucet of intercession given us by God, and obviously recognized by Saint Francis de Sales, who stated that whenever he was in dire need of prayer he invariably called upon someone who was in pain.

It has long seemed to me that redemptive suffering is one of the most awe-inspiring of all God's miracles. The trouble is that it is so rare. But those who know the healing Christ, those who with the Christian's sure and certain hope await their healing, can at the same time suffer redemptively.

There is nothing either morbid or contradictory in the healing ministry if, when you are suffering in any way, you pray that God will enable you to accept your suffering gladly, uniting it with our Lord's own perfect sacrifice. If we suffer in union with Him we have the inestimable privilege of sharing in a special way in the whole redemptive process. There can be a unique joy in offering our suffering on behalf of someone else who is in need of prayer. We have our scriptural authority for this in Saint Paul's words: "It is now my happiness to suffer for you. This is my way of helping to complete, in my poor human flesh, the full tale of Christ's afflictions still to be endured, for the sake of his body which is the church" (Col. 1:24 N.E.B.).

This is not to say that your suffering or mine has any *atoning* merit, for the Atonement belongs to Christ alone. He made the one full, perfect, and sufficient sacrifice for the sins of the world. No one of us can add to that. However, our suffering *does* lead to tne setting free of life to be imparted to others. The words "for the sake of his body which is the church" mean that there is no separation between helping Christ and helping the church—for union with Him means union with all those who are in Him.

Here we come to a great paradox: Accepting your suffering never means that you must not simultaneously seek to resist and overcome it in His name. Although God does not send disease and suffering, He permits it. Victory over it becomes a challenge to our courage and our trust

in Him. It is the test by fire, a test not willfully given by
God but abundantly blessed by Him when it is success
fully met. It is then that we hear in our hearts His
words, "In thee I am well pleased," and we know a great
joy, because by His grace, we have kept the faith.

The paradox involved here can by reconciled only by
the Holy Spirit. It is He who teaches us through Scripture and revelation that suffering from disease is an evil,
and that no man may desire it for its own sake. And yet
in offering it to God to be used on behalf of another it is
redeemed and thus becomes creative and constructive.

How do you offer your suffering? By praying something
like this: "Lord, I offer you my sins, my contrite heart,
my suffering, my entire life, such as it is—to be used for
Your glory—and please use it on behalf of John, whose
need is so great." If you so pray with your heart, He will
use your offering as you ask.

I remember well the young woman who came to Calvary for the first time in a wheelchair, her face white and
drawn, her body racked by the pain of cancer which no
drugs could alleviate. On that particular night I happened to speak of offering one's suffering on behalf of
another. The following week the young woman was back
again, this time her face radiant. She told me that she
had "practiced" all the preceding week the things I had
suggested. Not only was the friend for whom she offered
her pain healed, but she herself had dramatically
improved. "The thought that my suffering was not
wasted," she said, "but used by God to help someone
else, has made the difference. This knowledge is better
than a shot of morphine in so far as making one's own
pain endurable."

What happened in the case of this young woman
happens to many persons. We offer our suffering in union
with His, and not only are those for whom we pray
helped but, unsought and unasked, our own pain is very
frequently relieved. How this "works" is one of God's

greatest mysteries—but that it does work in many cases is beyond any doubt.

We learn from the Cross that all life is to be vicarious. Christ's sacrifice was for us a vicarious sacrifice; that is, He suffered in our stead. The offering of our suffering on behalf of another is, in a sense, God's vicarious sacrifice in continuing action, in which we have the great privilege of participating in an infinitesimal way, holding always before us this promise: "If we suffer we shall also reign with Him" (II Tim. 2:12).

During a group discussion a woman asserted rather belligerently, "The belief that suffering can be redemptive is man-made. There is nothing in Scripture to substantiate this idea."

In reply, I quoted to her: "Forasmuch then as Christ hath suffered in the flesh, arm yourselves likewise with the same mind: Rejoice, inasmuch as ye are partakers of Christ's sufferings" (I Pet. 4:1, 13).

Someone else in the group promptly retorted, "Then if we want to be really close to Christ, we should all seek pain."

No. To seek suffering in order to become more at one with Christ would be a prideful indulgence. One of the great saints of centuries ago who cruelly mortified his body confessed before he died that he believed he had been mistaken so to do, that he should have cared for, not virtually destroyed, his God-given body, the temple of the Holy Spirit.

There is a great difference between deliberately afflicting our bodies so that we may have more to offer God and constructively using the affliction we have while expectantly awaiting our healing which is His perfect will. It is said of Saint Teresa that during one period of her life she suffered from an ailment which made walking difficult, and yet she persisted each day in walking around the convent's spacious grounds. When asked why she did this, she replied, "I offer the pain to

God, praying that He will use it to lessen the weariness of a missionary I know."

The saint was actually enacting the words of Paul: "It is now my happiness to suffer for you. This is my way of helping to complete, in my poor human flesh, the full tale of Christ's afflictions still to be endured, for the sake of his body which is the church" (Col. 1:24 N.E.B.).

Throughout the day, when you offer your suffering to God on behalf of another in need, give thanks that He is using you as an instrument in imparting His life to His own household, the church. Then await with confidence the fullness of His healing power in your own life.

When night comes, remember these words of Saint Paul: "Never get tired of staying awake to pray for all the saints" (Eph. 6:18 Jer.). If you are sleepless for any reason, this is good advice not difficult to follow, and your very sleeplessness becomes one more thing you may gratefully offer. The curse of sleeplessness becomes a blessing if you use the long, still hours of the night not in cloying self-pity or restless tossing but in prayer on behalf of others who lie awake. As you offer your sleeplessness "for all the saints," you can be assured, although you do not know precisely how or why, that your intercessions will have great power, bringing comfort and solace to people you may not even know. And once again, unsought and unasked, will come to *you* a blessing. You will relax, cease twisting and turning, and lie quiet in His near presence. As you pray you will find great joy in the knowledge that you are somehow mysteriously mitigating the world's common suffering, as by sharing Christ's suffering you also share in His glory and thus become His true co-heir (Rom. 8:17).

"Such knowledge is too wonderful for me" (Ps. 139:6) will be your final thought. Committing your spirit and all those for whom you pray into His hands, you fall asleep.

Chapter 6

NOT MY WILL
BUT THINE

NOT LONG AGO I had a personal experience which simultaneously reinforced my conclusions and shed new light on why so many who sincerely claim that they desire healing so that they may better serve and witness to God's glory remain unhealed. At the same time I learned an invaluable lesson concerning unwitting presumption. Perhaps the reason this lesson had to be learned was that we who believe in the healing Christ are so unequivocally convinced that it is His perfect will that we be made whole that we are inclined to extend this certainty into areas where we cannot be equally sure of His will without a certain presumption.

The experience of which I speak had its beginning on a Monday night at Calvary, when in the healing-service meditation I spoke out strongly against the heresies so prevalent in the church today. I took for my text these words: "The Spirit speaketh expressly that in the latter times some shall depart from the faith, giving heed to seducing spirits, and doctrines of devils" (I Tim. 4:1). As

I spoke that night I was peculiarly conscious of a great blessing from God, a true anointing, so that it seemed to me it was not I who spoke but the Holy Spirit through my lips.

Filled with joy, I drove home after the service, thinking ahead to the mission I was scheduled to lead at the end of the week in another state. It was to be an extremely strenuous three days, and as I drove I thanked God that my back was now so much better.

The next morning, while dressing, I reached out to pick up an article on my dressing table, neither twisting nor bending in any way. As I picked the object up, I could hardly believe what happened: I felt that excruciating pain reminiscent of the airplane episode now five years in the past. This time it was even more severe. I gasped aloud the only prayer I could summon: "Christ have mercy."

I knew I should lie flat, but I was incapable of getting on my bed. Standing rigid, I called a friend and asked for prayer. I could not reach my physician, but my therapist agreed to take me at once. The immediate problem was how to get to his office. For no apparent reason I opened the nearby closet door. Looking up, I saw on the top shelf the long-forgotten cast in which I had been placed years before at the time of the original injury. With a prayer, I tentatively lifted my arms, managing to reach the cast. Laboriously I worked my way into it, and I called the custodian of my apartment, who drove me to the therapist.

Returning home after an agonizing trip to his office, I finally managed to get myself on the bed. There I lay, cast and all, for many hours.

Contemplating this freak "accident," there came a flash of recognition and I knew its source. I am well aware that many do not believe in Satan: I do, as surely as I believe in God. I recalled my meditation against heresy the preceding night and the blessing experienced from God; and I knew now that Satan had attacked again as he had so often in the past, and as he invariably does each time we come extremely close to God.

It is said that Satan is very clever, but my own experience leads me to think him abysmally stupid—for he never seems to learn that he cannot win. He can never reach those who love God through our bodies or in any other way, for in the end Christ is always triumphant.

I knew that day that there was a battle to be won, and engaged myself at that moment in the spiritual warfare of which Saint Paul speaks: "We wrestle not against flesh and blood, but against principalities, against powers, against the rulers of the darkness of this world" (Eph. 6:12). This is a challenge of which every Christian should be aware, and one from which he dares not shrink.

Reaching out for the cross on my bed table, clutching it so tightly that my palms bled, I said aloud, "In the name of Jesus I command you to leave me undisturbed." Knowing whom and what I was fighting, and in Whose name, gave me enormous strength.

At about midnight I struggled up to get a glass of water —a task that took me nearly an hour to accomplish. But it was the first step toward victory, for I was convinced that I could do all things through Christ. The remainder of the night I lay awake, in deep communion with God, and I was unafraid.

My great concern was the mission. It had been scheduled for over a year. I knew that in addition to the local people many were coming in from distant points. I simply could not disappoint all these people.

My attitude of prayer all that day and night had been, "Lord, I know it is Your will that I get to this mission. But I can't do it unless You get me on my feet. So please, Lord, raise me up."

The following morning I reached my physician, who hoped to inject the "pain points" with Novocain—but there were no "points." My entire back was involved. The only alternative seemed the hospital—I had been hospitalized before for far less—but hospitalization now was impossible because of the impending mission.

Later that day my rector brought me holy communion and anointed me. An hour later I felt curiously blessed, and so close to God I could not panic although I was still completely helpless and unable to move. Again and again I offered the pain to be used for His glory and on behalf of someone I knew who suffered. (This individual, incidentally, was healed of the pain of bursitis that same day.)

Saint Paul's words echoed and reechoed in my brain: "This is my way of helping to complete, in my poor human flesh, the full tale of Christ's afflictions still to be endured, for the sake of his body which is the church" (Col. 1:24 N.E.B.).

I began to feel a strange detachment from the pain, as if it were not my own but part of the world's pool of common suffering, a drop in the filling of the cup which in humility and with an inexplicable joy I could offer.

But it was now Wednesday night—perilously close to Friday morning, when I had to leave Pittsburgh. So again I prayed: "Lord, please raise me from this bed. You know I can't go anywhere in this condition."

Suddenly I received so strong an impression that it seemed as if I actually heard the words: "You are praying amiss." At that same instant I knew that the mission did not at all depend on my being there and that if I were unable to make it the pastor of the mission church would manage without me, for God would lead him to someone who would doubtless do a far better job than myself.

"When we know not how we should pray as we ought, the Holy Spirit maketh intercession for us—according to

the will of God" (Rom. 8:26, 27); and so now did He pray
in me: "Lord, I am not at all sure of Your will in this
matter. You alone know best how You will be glorified.
Forgive my presumption in believing that the mission
would suffer if *I* were not there to witness to Your glory.
Whether I am healed or not is entirely in Your hands. I
have only one desire: that not my will but Thine be done
in this whole matter."

As this prayer was concluded there was the momentary
shining of a brilliant light, and I saw the shadowed out-
line of an outstretched hand. Instinctively I raised mine
to meet it, and as I did so I heard in my heart these
words: "I the Lord thy God will hold thy right hand,
saying unto thee, Fear not; I will help thee" (Isa. 41:13).

A searing heat went through my body, and I broke out
in so heavy a sweat that my bedclothes were soaked. I
was still in severe pain and unable to get out of bed to
change them. I lay motionless on the drenched sheet, but
filled now with the assurance that I would be able to do
the mission.

Next morning I got out of bed with a minimum of pain.
I had my hair done, packed, took care of my always
voluminous correspondence, and felt better with each
passing hour. By Friday morning I was entirely well, and
I left on schedule to lead one of the most arduous missions
in which I have ever been privileged to participate.

It is God's perfect will that we be whole in every
respect, body, mind, and spirit. Our Lord taught us by
His earthly ministry the importance of physical healing.
He also taught us that the curing of the body is not of
primary importance; that our eternal destiny is not physical health, but holiness. "Ye shall be holy; for I am holy"
(I Pet. 1:16). A prerequisite to holiness is the complete
abandonment of our lives to Him. It is in this way that we
are most likely to receive physical healing.

How often in the past have I urged people to pray the prayer of relinquishment, and how often in the past have I prayed it myself. Yet in the situation I have just described it took me two days to realize my failure. In my assumption that God must heal me then and there in order that I might properly serve Him on the mission, I was unwittingly guilty of the sin of presumption. I had fallen into the trap of believing that I knew better than He how to serve and witness to Him most effectively. The truth is, that however strongly we may feel that by our healing we may be better servants of Christ, it is He who is the sole judge. It is He and He alone who knows whether He wants us to serve or simply to be. I have at last learned beyond the shadow of any doubt that if He wants us to serve, He will enable us to do so no matter how great our weakness, for with God nothing is impossible. His grace is always sufficient for the fulfillment of His will.

I have learned how mistaken we can be in our zeal to serve. It is our devotion to Him, our willingness to be used *by* Him and not necessarily *for* Him, that He most wants.

"Can ye drink of the cup that I drink of?" He asks (Mark 10:38). Like James and John, we answer quickly and without hesitation: "We can." But we are to discover that it is far more difficult to drink of the cup than to serve, and far easier to serve than to be poured out.

The mission was spectacularly powerful. Rarely have I seen so tremendous an outpouring of the Holy Spirit, the risen Christ present in all His glory and power.

In the past I have often commented on what I choose to call the spiritual law of difficulty. This law seemed to be operative so consistently that I believed it could not be pure happenstance, but rather the working out of a true spiritual law. The events of the past six years have changed what was personal opinion into a firm certitude. The more difficult it is for an individual to attend a healing service, the greater the sacrificial effort and expenditure of time involved, the greater the blessing to the supplicant. If you are disabled or in pain, if you come to healing services at personal cost, God will abundantly bless you—for in your effort, in spite of sacrifice or obstacle, you have performed an act of faith which is pleasing in His sight. This is one of the reasons I urge the sick and suffering to come in person to the Calvary weekly services when at all possible if their physician permits.

The healing ministry is at once the most subjective of all the ministries of the church and one of the most powerful instruments of intercession God has placed in our hands. The intercessions do not go unheard or unhonored by God, and for those too incapacitated to attend in person, intercession is sufficient. Many and marvelous are the healings so wrought, but whenever an individual is able to come on his own behalf, he should do so. This signifies the act of faith God desires of you and for which He blesses you.

At the same time, the more difficult circumstances are for the one who ministers, the more power seems to be released. I have cited illustrations in the past concerning the operation of this law as it has applied to me [1]—for example, the traveling over treacherous, icy roads to a hospital at two o'clock in the morning to see a patient and the leading of missions under extreme discomfort. However, the increased outpouring of the Holy Spirit under the conditions I had previously reported pales before the power released during more recent years when I have worked under a severe physical handicap, a handicap increased by late planes, torturously long lay-overs in airports, and bad weather.

[1] Emily Gardiner Neal, *Where There's Smoke* (New York: Morehouse-Barlow, 1967), p. 55.

On one occasion, for instance, the car placed at my disposal stalled, and I was forced to walk over half a mile in a blizzard, with the temperature (taking into account the chill factor) at forty degrees below zero. On another occasion it was necessary to travel to and from the mission church over snow banks so high that the compact car carrying me would crawl laboriously to the top of each bank, then drop back to the road with a jar calculated to break every bone in a human body! And long shall I remember being stranded (fortunately I was returning from a mission) in a snowed-in airport, standing in line six hours to change my ticket, and finally being housed in an airport motel room. Here I remained in total isolation for thirty hours, cut off from the dining room or any room service by an ice storm of unprecedented severity. And I recall as well suffocating in Midwest heat, with the thermometer at 106 degrees, and no air conditioning!

When three such experiences in a row were followed by two forced plane landings in rapid succession, each resulting in further injury to my spine, a friend, perhaps understandably, said to me, "Don't you think these continual difficulties and out-of-the-ordinary hardships are evidence that God wills you to stop leading missions?"

My answer was "No." While it was perfectly obvious that the life I was living was scarcely conducive to physical healing, and while it was equally clear that if I stopped working I would be spared much physical pain, I knew with every fiber of my being that it was God's will that I continue. It was with this knowledge that I realized most forcibly how erroneous is the impression given by many of us who work in the healing ministry that physical suffering is something to be avoided under all circumstances.

While we believe that pain is not the will of God, nevertheless there are times when we cannot do His will

without suffering. At such times there is no question of
choice: The transcendent desire is obedience no matter
what the cost. And it is a cost joyfully paid, for I have
learned over the past years that there are far worse
things than physical pain. I was compelled to go on; my
compulsion was the love of Christ. Some spoke of courage,
not realizing that my efforts took no courage whatsoever,
for had I been disobedient to what I knew in my heart
was the heavenly vision (Acts 26:19), the ensuing
spiritual anguish would have been intolerable. Furthermore, my ability to continue was in no way due to my
own willpower, as some have suggested. No willpower
that I could have summoned would have been sufficient.
It was only the imperative surrender of my own will,
which led in turn to complete dependency on Christ in
whom lies all strength, that made it possible for me to
go on.

My conviction of God's will in the matter was an inner
knowledge of the spirit, but one of the visible means for
my certainty lay in the overwhelming power released
during healing services when the going was especially
hard. The reason for this seems clear: In great physical
weakness one can do nothing on one's own. Thus He
and He alone led these missions.

And so it was with the mission mentioned earlier. I
knew it would be extraordinarily blessed: Not only had *I*
such difficulty getting there, but the church was filled
with the lame, the halt, and the blind, many of whom
had endured an extremely long bus ride to get to the
mission; all of these people had come at great sacrifice of
time, and most of them at great cost in terms of physical
pain.

The first healing was a dramatic one, of a type I have
seen with great frequency over the past several years. I
saw out of the corner of my eye a man walk up to the
altar rail with a brisk and unfaltering stride. He knelt

for the laying on of hands with prayer. As he walked back
to his pew, he was limping so badly that two ushers
rushed to his assistance. I have learned not to question
God, but I remember thinking, "God does *indeed* move
in mysterious ways"—for this man had walked to the
altar rail in perfectly normal fashion, and he left it
apparently crippled!

Later in the mission I learned what had happened. One
of this man's legs had been two inches shorter than the
other, so he was wearing a built-up shoe. At the altar
rail, his shortened leg had lengthened two inches and
was now equal with the other—hence the limp.

A young boy in a wheelchair, who had been paralyzed
and without speech since an automobile accident several
years before, regained considerable use of his limbs. In
the middle of the service he stood up in his chair and
spoke his first words since the accident: Loudly and
clearly he proclaimed, "Praise the Lord!"

Then there was the child with leukemia, a clergyman's
son. At the final healing service, as I prayed that the
Blood of Jesus flow through the body of this child, I had
the conviction that he was healed. Before leaving the
church that night I asked the father to administer holy
communion daily to his son, although the child was only
four. This he agreed to do. Several years after the mission,
the boy's disease has been, according to his physicians,
"in an unexpectedly long state of remission." This period
of remission has been unbroken since that final healing
service. Coincidence? I think not, in view of similar
long remissions of acute leukemia under similar
circumstances.

Of four retarded children for whom healing prayer was
offered, three have made continued progress toward
normalcy. Physical healings during the mission were
dramatic and numerous. Equally amazing was the healing of a young drug addict. For three days during the

mission he took no narcotics whatsoever. Although on hard drugs, he suffered no withdrawal symptoms, and he lost all craving. A follow-up for some months indicated that the healing was permanent.

In the same category was an alcoholic, whose wife was threatening to leave him and take their children. During the mission this man lost all desire for alcohol. A year later he had not had, nor did he wish to have, a drink.

Throughout the mission the church was vibrant with the presence of God. People were responding to His love in ways they did not themselves comprehend. They were performing the most extraordinary acts of kindness one for another; one young man drove 220 miles round trip between the afternoon and evening services to bring a relative of someone at the mission to the final healing service.

People were experiencing the supernatural love of God in an unprecedented, and to them unfamiliar, way. I vividly recall a registered nurse who, blind for four years, regained her sight. At the coffee hour following the final service this woman, tears of joy streaming down her face, told me how she had felt *my* love for her pour through her as I laid on hands.

"How could you so love a total stranger?" she asked me.

Of course, it was actually not *my* love but the love of Christ she had experienced. *I* did not even know I had laid hands on her until she told me.

The love of Christ washed over everyone there, healing not only bodies and emotions and spirits, but broken relationships of every kind. Typical of these was a broken marriage. The couple, who had already parted, were induced by friends to come to the mission. They came separately, sitting in different sections of the church, and at the first healing service came up to receive the healing rite at different times. At the second healing service they found themselves, surely through the work of the Holy Spirit, unexpectedly kneeling at the altar rail side by side. As prayers were offered that they might manifest to each other the love of Christ, the healing actually began. On the final night of the mission, they came to the service together, and they arose from their knees transfigured. I was to receive a letter several months later signed by both. It told me of their new-found happiness together in Christ, to Whom they have committed their lives. The Great Reconciler had done His work.

One of the healings for which I was most grateful was that of a woman in her early forties. I had noticed her each night being half-carried to the altar rail by friends. At the end of the mission I learned her story— not an uncommon one, but always wonderful to hear. She was in the terminal stages of cancer, and her physician had given her only a few weeks to live. She came to me at the conclusion of the final healing service, her face radiant, and said, "Mrs. Neal, you simply can't imagine my sheer terror of death. During this mission I have experienced the reality and the love of God. Now I no longer fear death, but I look forward to being wholly with my Lord with the same anticipation as a child on Christmas morning."

Whether this woman lived or died I do not know. But if she lived, she lives in Christ, and if she died, she died in Him, experiencing her healing in His own way— wherever and however He chose to heal.

That final healing service was indeed Christ triumphant. Every single person who came to the altar rail came to offer praise and thanksgiving to almighty God. Each and every one committed or recommitted his life to Christ as his Saviour and Redeemer. And this, of course, is what the healing ministry is all about, and this for me determines the "success" of a mission. Marvelous as are the physical healings, wonderful as are the healings in every area of life, the greatest of all healings and the greatest of all miracles is the conversion of the soul.

Chapter 7

HOLINESS AND WHOLENESS

DURING A RECENT MISSION an eighteen-year-old boy planning to enter the ministry asked me, "If someone were sufficiently holy, would he be sick?" At first glance this question may appear naïve, but in actuality it is extremely astute. Our subsequent discussion led into an area in which there is much confusion, an area too often left untouched by those of us in the healing ministry. As a result of this neglect, considerable unnecessary suffering is caused.

I explained to this young man that no one on earth is immune from illness, that as long as there is evil in the world, there will be suffering; and there will be evil on earth as long as man inhabits it.

Even as I spoke, I realized that too many people, lacking an adequate understanding of the healing ministry, tend to equate holiness with physical wholeness.

It is true that the words "holiness" and "wholeness" have a common root. Most certainly it is God's primary will that all of us be physically as well as spiritually

59

whole; otherwise, over one-third of the gospel would not be devoted to our Lord's earthly healing ministry. However, His perfect will is often circumvented by reasons beyond our individual control, such as the evil and unbelief of the world, of which we are all victims. That His primary will is temporarily deflected does not mean that an individual who happens to be physically ill cannot be gloriously whole in Christ.

There are many people like a woman I know who in her early forties is afflicted with a rare and devastating type of arthritis. This disease causes progressive crippling and unremitting, almost intolerable, pain. I was asked to minister to this woman, now bedridden. As I entered her room, there was no mistaking the radiance of Christ that shone from her eyes. She expectantly awaits her physical healing, but in the larger and most important sense she is even now whole in Christ. She dwells in Him, and He in her. To enter her presence was for me a benediction, as it is for all who know her.

The young man went on: "If holiness does not assure one's physical well-being, why do you speak continually of growing in grace and holiness, of the need to establish a closer union with God, so that physical healing may occur?"

The reason for my emphasis on this closer relationship with God, which obviously must result in increasing holiness, is this: The master key to all healing is found in the words "Seek ye first the kingdom of God." As Christians we do not seek physical health for health's sake; we are called to seek God for *His* sake, to seek Him above all else and for Himself alone. It is only then that we can reasonably expect that "all these things"—such as healing—"shall be added unto you" (Matt. 6:33).

The equation of holiness with physical health is untenable and does a grave disservice to the sick. One of the cruelest axioms I know, frequently quoted in the healing ministry, is; "There is no such thing as an incurable disease, only incurable persons." There is, to be sure, a half-truth here: There are indeed no incurable diseases in the sight of God. I have witnessed healings of virtually every disease known to man, many of them termed medically incurable. However, in the second part of this axiom, the clear—and mistaken—implication is that the *patient* is invariably responsible if healing fails to occur. This assumption is in direct opposition to the teaching of the ancient church, which did not ascribe such failure to the individual's lack of faith, but to the paucity of faith of the Body as a whole—which is to say, of the church.

Those who are suffering illness have enough with which to contend without adding an unjustifiable burden of guilt. It is a well-known fact that the sick frequently suffer from guilt feelings simply because they are sick. It is a peculiar psychological truth that non-Christians also harbor guilt feelings during an illness, possibly because they feel they are causing their families worry and expense. Perhaps the prevalence of guilt feelings during illness comes from the fact that buried deep in the unconscious of many individuals, Christian or not, is the erroneous idea promulgated by the church for so many centuries that God sends sickness as a punishment.

Christians who believe wholeheartedly in the healing Christ are prone to feel the guiltiest of all. Some of us who work in the healing ministry, including myself, must assume responsibility for at least part of the emotional suffering the believer too often endures. We state categorically—and correctly—that sickness is *not* the primary will of God. But there is danger in this teaching if we do not expand upon it. It is fatally easy for the sick to misunderstand, to wonder if, because they are ill, they are really in the will of God at all.

As one woman put it, "I have cancer, and I am seeking the healing power of God. However," she went on, "if His will is complete wholeness of body, mind, and spirit, does the fact that I am now physically sick mean that I am not in His will?" Then she added in a strained voice, "And suppose I am *not* healed here and now?"

This woman was a committed Christian. Her concern was not motivated by fear of continued physical pain, but rather by her extreme apprehension that if she were *not* healed it would mean she was outside the will of God.

For years I have observed this kind of apprehension among the sick who are dedicated to the healing Christ. It touched even an outstanding leader in the healing field who, stricken with a deadly disease, felt himself abandoned by God.

After extensive and intensive counseling among such individuals, during which I was able, I believe successfully, to allay their fears, I felt greatly blessed when I was injured—for my own suffering was not now compounded by feelings of guilt or confusion. Nevertheless, because of my personal experience I understand more clearly than ever before how such gross misapprehensions can occur. At the same time, I am now even more certain, because of empirical knowledge, that whether sick or well we are all safely held in the palm of God's hand, and He will never let us fall. I can say with complete assurance that you are most certainly in the center of His will if you are praying in faith for your total wholeness—for you are then praying according to His holy will.

If many Christians suffer needless guilt over their illnesses, there are likewise many who, as they await their healing, may be enduring great physical pain. Added to this there is frequently the mental anguish caused by the fallacious thought that they are somehow "letting God down" and proving themselves poor Christians if they acknowledge or dare to admit that they are suffering.

I have spoken earlier of the wonder of true redemptive suffering, and of how God can use your pain so that it becomes creative and productive. But pain of itself and for itself does not ennoble. It tends rather to demoralize, the patient becoming irritable and disagreeable. If sufficiently severe, pain can temporarily degrade the most spiritual among us to a purely animalistic level.

I know a wonderful Christian woman who is now extremely elderly and ill. Instead of possessing the tranquillity of old age, she is often cantankerous and querulous. She abhors this in herself, and constantly pleads for prayer that God may enable her in her suffering to be the sort of person He would want her to be. In truth she *is* that person: a devout and godly woman, whose spirit has been briefly trapped by her body.

Each individual has a different threshold of pain, some higher than others through no virtue of their own; some lower, through no personal fault. Those who are able to stand pain less well than others should feel neither guilty nor ashamed if they are making every effort to unite their suffering with Christ.

I remember that a long time ago, before I understood these things as I do now, how stupidly disillusioned I was when I witnessed the suffering of a great spiritual leader. I saw this man of God become against his will, though only for a short time, a demoralized wreck. In my ignorance I had the temerity to judge him. I did not comprehend then that the man I was watching was not, just for a little while, his true self. For the moment his pain had become a live and evil thing that simply appeared to my then-blind eyes to have taken him over. At the end, this saintly man died with a smile, the holy name of Jesus on his lips. Since then I have come to know that there can be intervals in the lives of the most courageous and godly people when pain seems to transcend all else. It only *seems* this way, for we are human as well as spiritual beings; and the suffering attacks our humanity, not our spirit, which is unscathed.

During our lifetime we all will suffer to a lesser or greater degree. You should feel no guilt if your cry "Lord, save" is involuntarily interrupted by the scream for physical help that seems to come from outside yourself: "Nurse—give me a hypodermic." Our Lord understands. Again we know the wonder of the Incarnation, for He has traversed the road of pain before us.

Before I was a Christian, one of the chief reasons for my agnosticism was the pain and suffering of all kinds I saw abounding in the world. Where was this merciful God of whom Christians were continually prating?

Finally I came to understand that it is not God but man who is responsible for war, for the hungry, for the deprived, for all social injustice. At long last I came to comprehend that one of God's greatest gifts to us is that of free will, but we have made of it a curse by its abuse.

"I have loved you, saith the Lord. Yet ye say, Wherein hast thou loved us?" (Mal. 1:2). One of the most compelling apologetics for the Christian faith so far as I am concerned has been my observation (and now my personal experience) that those who suffer most, in whatever areas of their lives, are usually the most aware of the love of God.

I think of a short time ago when after I had spoken in a church, one of the congregation came up to me, almost startlingly alight with the love of Christ. He then proceeded to tell me something of his life, and once again I marveled.

He had a twenty-year-old daughter who lay in an institution, as helpless as a six-month-old baby. His wife had committed suicide the year before. He had come to the church this night, seeking the healing power of God for his young son who suffered from leukemia. Surely, from a purely human viewpoint, this man had every reason to feel bitter and God-forsaken; yet the reverse was true. He spoke not in self-pity, but in gratitude for the love of God, which continually filled and upheld him. This the unbeliever cannot understand, but the Christian never doubts. He knows in his own life the truth of the words of French theologian Louis Evely: "When we suffer, the Father follows us with His eyes, with the same solicitude, the same admiration, the same anxious tenderness, the same wish to rescue and to help as when He looked on the Son as He went towards His Cross." [1]

Many of us do not fear death, but only the suffering we may have to endure in the process of dying. I vividly recall a woman who came to me directly after receiving her physician's verdict that her entire body was riddled with cancer. She said, "I know that Christ will heal me— if not here on earth, then when I am wholly with Him. The only thing I really fear is the suffering, for I know I don't bear pain well."

This woman suffered greatly, but I recall how often she received the laying on of hands with prayer, and how often her pain was either marvelously diminished or entirely eliminated for increasingly long periods of time. This is the mercy of God.

None of us understands the mystery of pain, suffering, and disease. Our Lord made no attempt to explain it. He simply healed, making crystal clear that it was not of the kingdom of God (Luke 13:16). He has given us the means of grace to combat the enemy: prayer, sacrament, and the healing rites. When we use these God-given means, we invariably receive from Him either surcease from pain or the strength to withstand it—and very often the gift of complete healing.

Although the fact that we are Christians does not mean that we shall not ever have to suffer, it *does* mean that with each respite from pain we as Christians can cry, "Save me, O Lord," and we shall be saved; we can cry, "Christ have mercy," and He will.

[1] Louis Evely, *We Dare to Say Our Father* (New York: Herder and Herder, 1965), p. 94.

The demoralization severe pain can cause is a transient thing. In the eyes of God it can and will be transcended by our inner knowledge, which never wavers, that Jesus is always with us. As we grasp His healing hand despite the pain, we are aware that we are safe within His providence, that in Him lies our healing if only we will hang on.

We know beyond the shadow of any doubt that in *everything* God works for good with those who love Him (Rom. 8:28 R.S.V.), and that nothing can ever separate us from His love. Though our lips may cry out in pain, our hearts are quiet in the serene knowledge that God will not let us suffer more than we are able to bear (I Cor. 10:13). Because our Lord suffered, He knows how we feel and why. He felt and endured all that we feel and endure, for He was like us in all ways, except that He was without sin (Heb. 4:15).

If, then, you suffer while you await your healing, if your body seems held in a vise of pain like an animal in a steel trap, don't feel ashamed or guilty if momentarily your desire for relief of pain seems to supersede your desire for God. Your body may be temporarily trapped, but your spirit will soar joyously free, made so by Christ. Remember always that *nothing* can wrest you from His everlasting arms. In this knowledge lies His peace and joy, which He makes yours.

It is said that Pope John XXIII wondered whether he would suffer well when his time of tribulation came. By God's grace he endured magnificently, suffering in union with the Lord he loved. The words of one of his meditations when he lay dying [2] have been of inestimable comfort to me under many different circumstances. I have made them my own as I lay in pain; I have prayed them for my church, for my nation, for those who suffer, for all people everywhere. If you are suffering in any way;

[2] Pope John XXIII, *Prayers and Devotions* (New York: Doubleday & Co., Image Books, 1969), p. 328.

if you pray for others and for the world, perhaps you will find them a source of comfort and inspiration as have I.

> This bed is an altar; the altar requires a victim: I am ready. I offer my life for the Church, for the peace of the world and the union of all Christians. The secret of my priesthood is to be found in the Crucifix I placed before my bed. He looks at me and I speak to Him. In our long and frequent conversations at night, the thought of the redemption of the world has seemed to me more urgent than ever before. I have other sheep that are not of this fold (John 10:16). His outstretched Arms show us that He died for all, for *all.* No one is denied His love and forgiveness. My earthly day is drawing to a close. But Christ lives and the Church continues on her way. Oh the souls, the souls of men. May they be one! May they be one!

Chapter 8

THE JOY OF THE LORD

IN A GROUP DISCUSSION not long ago, a man asserted that he and his wife had committed their lives to Christ, as had one of their grown daughters.

"However, my other daughter," he said, "who is married and lives far from home, is not the least interested in God or anything pertaining to Him."

When I asked if he knew why this was so, he replied, "Because she and her husband love fun and gaiety. They are afraid if they become real Christians it will mean the end of the way of life they so enjoy."

What a tragic mistake it is to think that to follow Jesus, to commit one's life to Him, means the end of all fun and enjoyment. The life of the spirit is the most exciting life on earth; one never knows what is around the corner in the way of revelation. The individual who is open to God is continually being astonished at the marvelous things He has in store for each one of us, and at the thrilling and wonderful way in which He works out His plan in our lives. To attempt to walk in the spirit is not only exciting, but fun and sheer joy, as an increasing number of young people are discovering.

One of the most gratifying things to me in leading the ongoing ministry of healing at Calvary Episcopal Church has been the opportunity to watch people grow, not only in holiness, but in pure, unadulterated joy.

As we bid each other goodnight at the end of the service, each face is aglow as he or she tells me of blessings received; invariably there are a number who report healings that have occurred. The atmosphere is pervaded with thanksgiving and joy, for all there have asked in His name; they have received; and as He promised, their joy is full (John 16:24). The congregation is loath to leave the church, and as the people stand around in groups speaking together of the wonder of the living Christ, their happiness overflows.

This is not to say that the healing ministry has a monopoly on committed, joy-filled Christians; yet with few exceptions, those who believe in the healing Christ are uniquely and joyously dedicated. They have seen demonstrated the stupendous truth that the kingdom is not a matter of talk but of power (I Cor. 4:20 N.E.B.), and they know beyond the shadow of a doubt that Christ is a tremendous power within them (II Cor. 13:3 Phillips).

A young woman who lives in a midtown apartment house and comes regularly to the Calvary services told me of an episode that gladdened my heart. She said that when she had returned home from a healing service the preceding week, one of her neighbors happened to be sitting in the lobby as she walked in. The neighbor looked at her and remarked, "You must have been to a great party tonight, you look so happy. Where was it, anyway?"

When the reply young woman answered, "I was at the healing service at Calvary," her neighbor was astounded. To see someone come home from a church service radiant and bursting with joy seemed completely incredible.

Yet this is the way it *should* be. A long face and mournful demeanor is a travesty of Christianity. A doleful attitude has nothing whatsoever to do with reverence: It is a hangover from Puritanism, which has no rightful place, nor ever had, in the Christian faith. If our sins continue to crucify Christ, so must the dour, joyless Christian break the heart of God.

There was nothing "wrong" with that young woman who loved gaiety and parties. So, apparently did Jesus, as we remember Him at the wedding feast at Cana (John 2:1–10). Not only do we assume that He had a good time, but He wanted the guests to enjoy themselves also. When the wine ran out, He turned the water into wine, and the festivities continued unabated.

Saint Paul encourages us to enjoy all things. As he says, they have been given us by God, "Who giveth us richly all things to enjoy" (I Tim. 6:17). How sad it is that so many Christians seem to find so little to enjoy in God's good gifts. God calls us to be holy, yes; but holiness and joy should be synonymous for the Christian. Too often they are not, which is why a young woman who came to me for counseling rebelled when I suggested she attend healing services.

"I don't want to," she said. "Why should I go to a place filled with forbidding, 'holy' people, all miserable, sick and unhappy. I'm depressed enough myself," she continued, "without being subjected to *that* atmosphere."

I finally prevailed upon her at least to try a healing service. She quickly discovered how wrong she had been, and now she never misses a service. She found not "forbidding, 'holy'" people, but the joy of the Lord. She now lives in this joy and abundantly manifests it to others.

A number of people fly in from various states to attend the Calvary services, and without exception they have all expressed the very same thought in differing words: "I have never felt such joy and love as at this service. It is an experience I shall never forget." They have experienced the meaning of the fellowship of the people of God.

Christian joy goes far beyond pleasure, gaiety, and happiness, although it may well include all three; and it is not marked by a saccharine sweetness and a false and forced cheeriness. Many of us would agree with the British writer and theologian Charles Williams when he says, "There is an offensive cheerfulness encouraged by some Christians which is very trying to any person of moderate sensibility." [1]

True joy is one side of the Christian coin; on the other is suffering. Unless we share in the common suffering of the world which is also the suffering of our Lord, we cannot enter into His joy. The early Christians went to their deaths singing joyous hymns of praise. As it was their joy in the face of persecution and martydom which resulted in the conversion of many pagans two thousand years ago, so it is this same joy that effects conversion today. The unbeliever observes the committed Christian and says, "I want what he has," and "what he has," of course, is the Lord Jesus Christ.

"Rejoice in the Lord always, and again I say rejoice," Paul enjoins us (Phil. 4:4). These are words of healing, for in the joy of the Lord does indeed lie our strength (Neh. 8:10). It is this joy that undergirds all true worship, that leads us into heartfelt thanksgiving and ceaseless praise, that underlies our intercessions (for part of our joy is our knowledge that God hears and answers prayer). It underlies even our penitence, for there is inestimable joy in our certitude that He never fails to forgive.

"For the kingdom of God is not meat and drink; but righteousness, and peace, and joy in the Holy Ghost" (Rom. 14:17).

These three—righteousness (or at least our striving toward it), peace, and joy—are inseparable and indivisible, for peace without joy degenerates into mere passivity, and righteousness without joy becomes prideful arrogance.

"Except a man be born again, he cannot see the king-

[1] Charles Williams, *He Came Down from Heaven* (London: Faber and Faber, 1950), p. 96.

dom of God" (John 3:3), and the fullness of His joy can be found only within the kingdom—that kingdom which is at once within us and yet to come (Luke 17:21).

"How can a man be born again?" asked Nicodemus (John 3:4). We ask the same question today, and the answer is the same as that given two thousand years ago: "Except a man be born of water and of the Spirit," Jesus says, "he cannot enter into the kingdom of God" (John 3:5).

Here our Lord enunciates the formula of Christian baptism as He proclaims the necessity of a spiritual regeneration "of water and of the Spirit." In His reply to Nicodemus He seems to make it clear that such baptism is necessary for salvation. Thus the majority of churches teach that in the sacrament of baptism we *are* born again, cleansed of sin, spiritually regenerated by the action of the Holy Spirit, and made members of the Body of Christ.

None of the sacraments, including baptism, is magic. If, as is the custom in many of the established churches, we are baptized as infants and live our entire adult lives apart from God and in sin, the fact that we were baptized will not save us, nor will the fact that as baptized Christians we may give lukewarm assent to whatever portions of the gospel we choose to believe, live by the Golden Rule and attend church every Sunday. It is necessary, as our Lord made clear, that we be *consciously* aware that we have been born again, or more accurately, born from above of God.

What then is this rebirth experience? What actually happens, and how does it affect us?

For the purpose of simplification, rebirth can be equated with conversion. The two are not precisely the same, because the word "conversion" as we use it generally applies to someone who has never known Christ, while the new-birth experience applies most often to those who have known and believed in Him, but less than completely. Nonetheless, conversion and rebirth have much in common. When the experience of rebirth occurs suddenly and dramatically there is an unforgettable moment of glorious truth, occasioned by the strong action of the Holy Spirit, when one accepts *entirely*— not just with his mind, but with his heart and spirit and his whole being—the stupendous fact that Jesus is indeed *his* personal Saviour and Redeemer. It is in this moment that the individual recognizes the extent of his sins, experiences the miracle of God's absolving grace, and commits his life utterly and without reservation to his Lord. The grace of the Holy Spirit, Whom you received in baptism, is conveyed now in a new and fuller way. You are enabled to claim, appropriate, exercise, and prepare to develop your relationship with God already established in baptism. If the new life in Christ is to be lived, there must be a "new" creature to live it, and we cannot become "new creatures" on our own; we must be reborn by the power of the Spirit. This is the sort of rebirth Jesus was talking about to Nicodemus.

When this new birth takes place, the born-again Christian knows experientially the reality of God and of His love, and the redemptive grace of Christ. He has appropriated the gift of the Holy Spirit promised by Saint Peter (Acts 2:38, 39) and received in baptism. This experiential knowledge of your spirit given by the Spirit may come in a variety of ways. Don't expect everyone's experience to be exactly like yours.

Very frequently there will be an exquisitely precise moment of truth. If this happens to you, it will be an experience without parallel in your life. It is in that moment that you will know not only with your mind but with your heart the complete holiness of God: His love for *you*, personally, and the lengths to which He has gone to prove His love by His Crucifixion. You will find yourself overwhelmed with your love for *Him* and with sorrow for your sins. Your heart will cry, "Lord, forgive, I am not worthy. Take me, all that I am, my life in its entirety, and use it as You will, for Your glory." You will simultaneously experience the greatest joy you have ever known. You will rise from your knees a new creature in Christ (II Cor. 5:17).

"Except a man be born again, he cannot see the kingdom of God." You have now been reborn, and you have glimpsed the kingdom. Your rebirth has happened within you, but it will be vividly apparent to all who know you.

Although the new-birth experience often occurs suddenly and dramatically, there are many for whom it is a gradual and scarcely perceptible awakening. These individuals cannot pinpoint in time the moment when they became aware of the reality of Jesus Christ and embraced not only His teachings but Himself. So far as they can remember, these persons have always known and accepted with joy their relationship with God. In other words, their baptism, at whatever age it occurred, "took."

It cannot be overemphasized that the born-again experience need not necessarily involve an instantaneous emotional reaction. I remember well a young woman who publicly committed her life to Christ at a Faith at Work religious conference. She came to me afterward, almost in tears, because she had not "felt" anything; she had heard no angels sing and no bells ring as she committed her life.

I saw this young woman over a year later. Just a few weeks before, she had experienced the sorrow for sin, the peace and indescribable joy, the experiential knowledge of Christ as her Saviour, which are characteristic of the born-again Christian. She was aglow with His radiance, and she said, "You know, my life is entirely different now."

Of course it was; old things had passed away, and all things had become new (II Cor. 5:17). She had been reborn into the joy of the Lord.

Each one of us experiences and is given to appropriate

in a different way that new life in Christ which became ours at baptism. The important thing to realize is this: Even if our born-again experience comes to us as a great flash of lightning, even if we know the precise instant when we were made new in Him, this experience is never a static thing. No Christian ever "has it made," for our "Yes" to Christ is a continuous and ongoing process that will never cease as long as we live.

"If thou shalt confess with thy mouth the Lord Jesus, and shalt believe in thine heart that God hath raised him from the dead, thou shalt be saved" (Rom. 10:9). This means far more than an exciting subjective religious experience, and it means far more than an intellectual assent to the fact that Christ was born, lived, was crucified, and rose again. It is only when the *heart* believes, and the *spirit* responds and *continues* to respond, that one is born from above.

It is worth noting that one of the outstanding characteristics of the healing ministry which is in no small part responsible for the power released and the joy experienced during healing services is the predominantly large number of reborn Christians associated with this ministry. The reason for this is not difficult to determine: Christ is within us (immanent) and at the same time outside us (transcendent). In a special way and with unique vividness, we confront the living God at the altars of His healing church. One cannot experience such a confrontation without being born anew in Him; and one cannot emerge from such a confrontation without becoming, in some way, a new creature.

It is through the new birth experience, wherever, whenever, and however it may come about, that we enter into the joy of the Lord. Believing now in a new way with a new fervency, we "rejoice with joy unspeakable" (I Pet. 1:8). With the Psalmist we say, and mean it with all our being, "In thy presence is fulness of joy; at thy right hand there are pleasures for evermore" (Ps. 16:11).

Chapter 9

"WILT THOU BE MADE WHOLE?"

AMONG THE FACTORS that inhibit God's healing power is one so prevalent, so important, and withal so insidious, that it deserves a chapter to itself. I refer to the lack of desire to be healed. To fail to *want* to be well is in itself a sickness, which has its scriptural counterpart in the gospel account of the healing of the man at Bethesda (John 5:2–17).

Here we see an ill person who gives Jesus one flimsy excuse after another as to why he has not been healed. Our Lord immediately understands the true situation and asks of the sick man, "Wilt thou be made whole?" (John 5:6)—in other words, "Do you *want* to be well again?"

This is a question I believe many ailing people must ask themselves today and search their hearts for an honest answer. "But," you may be thinking, "surely no one can *want* to be sick, or hold resentments, or suffer from poor relationships either at home or in business."

Unfortunately, as I have learned over the years, a great many people who ostensibly seek healing for whatever brokenness may exist in their lives *do* want things to remain precisely as they are. They do *not* honestly want themselves or the situation healed. This lack of real desire to have their lives made whole is usually unconscious, and therefore such individuals frequently need outside help to bring it to their conscious awareness.

But bringing it to their conscious mind is only the first step. From there on the major and most important portion of their healing consists in changing their frame of mind so that they truly desire health and wholeness. This is the most difficult part of the healing, but by God's grace it can be achieved. Once a person sincerely wants to be made whole in Christ's name and for His sake, the healing is virtually accomplished. The ailment to which he has clung, perhaps for years, whether it be physical, mental, or emotional, is very apt to quickly disappear.

A typical example concerns a woman who, when she was widowed, went to live with her daughter and son-in-law. They loved her deeply and genuinely wanted her with them. They owned a large house where she could be made comfortable and enjoy, both for their sakes and her own, a modicum of privacy.

This woman was not elderly. She was in her middle fifties, and her health had previously been excellent. However, within a few weeks after moving into her daughter's home, she began to ail. She became miserably and genuinely ill, although her physician could find nothing organically wrong with her. She finally came to the point where she had to spend most of her time in bed. She could eat virtually nothing without suffering acute discomfort, became very weak, and suffered from almost total insomnia. (Let me remark here that whether an illness is psychosomatic or organic makes no difference so far as suffering is concerned. Psychosomatic illness is just as real, just as painful, just as incapacitating, as organic sickness.)

It was this woman's daughter and son-in-law who, greatly concerned, asked me to see her. By the end of our first session, I felt I had put my finger on the problem. Like any widow under similar circumstances, she had formerly run her own home, in her case for more than thirty years. The adjustment to living in someone else's house was a difficult one: perhaps more difficult for her because she was extremely determined that she not be accused of "interfering." She was therefore under constant tension, fearful of expressing any contrary opinion. It was an unnatural and inhibited way of life, which no one could live indefinitely without detriment.

Now these things were contributing factors to her condition, but they were not the real reason for her sickness. The real reason was this: The most difficult adjustment a widow or a widower has to make is to the fact that no matter how devoted the children or grandchildren, no matter how loving other relatives and friends, a bereaved spouse is no longer first in anyone's life. The woman I speak of simply had not been able to make this most difficult emotional adjustment.

In talking with me she was embarrassed and apologetic; she blamed no one but herself. With her rational mind she would have had it no other way, but emotionally she had been unable to accept the fact that, as much as her daughter loved her, the daughter's husband had to come first in her life.

This woman had not been an overly possessive or demanding mother, but now, in an unconscious effort to come first in someone's life, she had become ill in order to focus attention on herself. She did not *want* to be well, for if she were, she felt she would be of less concern to her children.

This was clear to me from the beginning, but not to her, and had I pointed it out on that first visit she would have vehemently denied it. She might well have become angry and hostile toward me, most likely refusing to see me again, and thus I would have been powerless to help her. I prayed with her that first afternoon without laying on hands, asking the guidance of the Holy Spirit for both of us.

During the next few weeks the burden of my prayer at home for her was not for her physical cure, but that her neurosis might be healed by the love of God so that she would truly *want* to be well.

I saw her over a period of some six weeks, and toward the end of our last conference, she broke down and cried, she *herself* admitted what I had felt to be the trouble the first time I saw her.

During that final session together we prayed, this time with the laying on of hands, asking God to heal the brokenness of her spirit, praying that God's love would be so real to her that she would no longer need to feel "first" among those on earth. Our prayer was answered with a great affirmation of a Christian truth: that although God has so many millions of children, each one of us is to Him as special as though he were His only child —and, as such, all-important in His sight.

Within days this woman was amazingly better. Within two weeks, although formerly an irregular churchgoer, she began to attend church each Sunday and a healing service once a week. She is well now, but continues (as she should) to attend weekly healing services. She does this for several reasons, among them because, as she puts it, "When I receive the laying on of hands, it is as though our Lord Himself is touching me. I know the reality of His presence and His love at healing services as at no other time. I know there that I am His."

There are many like this woman who subconsciously do not want to be healed; but there are also some who, not understanding the healing ministry, *dare* not seek the healing power of God. There are those who suffer from a medically incurable disease, and with enormous spiritual effort have made peace with their situation. They are afraid to seek Christ's healing touch lest they not be physically cured. They cannot face the prospect of fighting all over again the battle of acceptance they have already won. In cases like this, I suggest that, except for private prayer, well-meaning enthusiasts of the healing ministry do not interfere.

To the question "Wilt thou be made whole?", which I seldom ask directly, I often add *very* directly, "Why do you want to be healed? What will you do with your life if you *are* healed?"

Not long ago I asked this of a woman whose arm, broken ten weeks before, was not healing. Her answer came swiftly, and, I thought, a little too glibly. "I'll devote the rest of my life to the glory of God," she said.

Week after week she came to the Calvary healing services, and I could see no evidence of either physical or spiritual healing taking place.

The last time she counseled with me she spoke continually of a trip to Europe she had long planned and now would have to cancel. Suddenly I found myself saying, "Look, let's examine your motives. Do you really want to be healed so that God will be glorified, or so that you can go to Europe?"

She looked nonplused for a moment, then burst out: "I want that trip to Europe more than anything else in the world. I couldn't care less about the glory of God!"

Here then was the trouble spot. It was not so much that her motives were wrong as that she had been dishonest with God—for it is honesty that He honors, not a false piety. That day she prayed with me, telling God how she *really* felt. Obviously, *He* did not need this information, but *she* needed to give it. The result? Her arm healed within ten days, and she went to Europe as planned, overwhelmed with gratitude to God. I heard from others that throughout the trip she made a moving and powerful witness to her Lord.

"Wilt thou be made whole?" Surely implicit in our Lord's question to the man at Bethesda was "How *much* do you want to be well?"

This is the question I am still asking a businessman who claims he wants to be healed, but apparently not sufficiently to remove the barriers which are impeding the inflow of God's healing grace.

This man, in his forties, has worked for the same firm for many years. Two years ago he was passed over for a promotion which he believed he merited. He is particularly bitter because the man who is now his superior had a drinking problem. Had it not been for the man I am counseling, who covered for his boss again and again, the man would have lost his job instead of being promoted. This is an understandable reason for resentment on the part of the subordinate, but he makes no effort to release it; rather, he appears to embrace it. The resentment has, in a sense, become a reason for his being. When I have tried to point out how he is harming himself, his reply is "Yes—but it is only human to resent this injustice."

Exactly so, which is why we must continually strive to be rid of such human sins of the spirit, and this can only be done by opening our hearts to the supranatural love and grace of God. This man initially came to me seeking healing for a physical ailment, but thus far I have been unable to help him, for he has shut himself off from God's healing power. God coerces no one, and this man, for the time being, has freely chosen to take no corrective measures, but instead to make his resentment a way of life. I am still working with him, confident that in the end the healing Christ will triumph, that in due time his spiritual ears will be unstopped and his spiritual eyes opened, that he may hear and see the truth.

Not long ago, he said with a grin, "You never give up, do you?" No, I don't, for at long last I have learned patience—an attribute which as Christians we should all try to cultivate, for we are dealing not only with the now but with all eternity. Great patience is particularly necessary for people who reject their healings, for whatever reason: Patience will allow them time for self-examination, and if required, extensive counseling, so that they may learn to live in a climate conducive to healing.

Once we have learned this, we all may be assured that we are growing, however slowly, in grace and holiness. We all can be certain that we shall be healed spiritually, so that we may truly want to be well. When that time comes, the chances are excellent that we shall receive the healing of which we are in need, whether it be physical, mental, or emotional.

Many of us would agree with Saint Teresa that patience is near the top of the list of Christian virtues, and that the painfulness of its acquisition is one of mankind's greatest crosses. Particularly is this true of us who live in this day and age, for we are members of what is probably the most impatient era in history. We are a generation of "instant" everything, from instant coffee to instant religious experience. However, there is no short cut to the fulfillment of the kingdom of God. The road to holiness is a long one, and we do not stop traveling when we are healed. We continue along it for the rest of our lives, blessed every step of the way by the Light of the world, by whom the path is lit.

It is true of all of us, and particularly of those who at one time may have rejected His healing grace, that once having tasted God, we are impatient and eager for more; there is born in us that holy desire which comes from God. But we cannot receive all of Him all at once, or indeed all of Him ever on this earth. He in His wisdom gives us what we can handle at a given time. Too much too soon can dangerously unbalance us emotionally.

Therefore, cultivate assiduously that fruit of the spirit called patience (Gal. 5:22 Jer.). When you seek healing, make sure you really want to be healed. If you even faintly suspect that in your heart you are enjoying your illness, or if you know that you are clinging to a sin of the spirit, ask God to release you from it. Pray that He will heal your spirit, and instill in you a genuine desire to be whole. He will answer your prayer, and the chances are good that your physical healing will follow.

Finally, be honest with God concerning your motive for healing. Don't pray piously, in a bargaining spirit: "Please, God, heal me, and I'll give you my life," when what you really mean is, "Heal me, God, so that I can go to that party two weeks from Saturday."

When you are unsure of your motives, one of the most effective prayers for healing I know, taken from the Book of Common Prayer, is, "Almighty God, unto whom all hearts are open, all desires known, and from whom no secrets are hid; Cleanse the thoughts of our hearts by the inspiration of thy Holy Spirit, that we may perfectly love thee, and worthily magnify thy Holy Name, through Christ our Lord." If we pray this prayer frequently and sincerely, we are likely to hear in our hearts the words of Jesus that were spoken to the sick man at Bethesda: "Rise, take up thy bed, and walk" (John 5:8).

And very likely it shall be with us, as it was with him: "And immediately the man was made whole, and took up his bed, and walked" (John 5:9).

Chapter 10

FAITH AND THE KINGDOM

"How CAN I ACQUIRE the faith necessary for healing?" is a perpetual question and at times one of obsessive concern to those to whom the healing ministry is new (or not so new, for that matter).

A simplistic answer is "You can't acquire faith; it is a gift of God. Your task is merely to appropriate that already-given gift."

But how do you do this? The first step is to realize the nature of faith, for the word "faith" is bandied about by all and sundry as though it were some sort of magic formula that of itself can heal. The fact is that faith of itself never healed anyone. It is God who heals, and faith that releases His power in our lives.

"What must I do to be saved?" asked the jail keeper of Paul and Silas (Acts 16:30). The reply came swiftly: "Believe on the Lord Jesus Christ." Substitute the word *healed* for *saved* in the question, and the answer is the same: Believe on the Lord Jesus Christ.

His miracles, accomplished by the power of the Holy

Spirit both when He walked the earth and today, are acts of mercy and evidence of His compassion. They are also signs witnessing to the kingdom He came to bring in. This is why He cannot work miracles unless He finds that quality of faith without which the signs and wonders, both two thousand years ago and now, lose their significance.

The possession of miracle-working faith demands in so far as is humanly possible the yielding of the whole person to God. This in turn requires an act of humility very difficult to perform, especially among us "do-it-yourself" Americans. Many people decline to make this act; more attempt it in half-hearted fashion, wanting the crown of healing without the cross of self-surrender. And total surrender to almighty God is a cross on which we must continually crucify ourselves if we are to be able to say with Saint Paul: "Not I, but Christ, liveth in me" (Gal. 2:20).

Some months ago a man came to me who had staggering problems, emotional, physical, and spiritual. At the same time, his marriage was on the rocks. He went to church regularly, knew his Scripture with his mind but not with his heart, and he was quick to admit that he was only a lip-service Christian. But he had a truly sincere desire to know his Lord.

"I *want* to believe with my heart that Jesus is my Lord and Saviour," he said, "but I just can't. My mind gets in the way no matter how hard I try."

This man actually spoke for many, and I tried to explain as I have so often before that in the area of faith, as in all other areas of our spiritual lives, it is our *wills* that God wants first. If we *will* to believe in our Lord with all our hearts, and if our overriding desire is for more of God, He will honor our will and desire for total commitment to Him.

To this man I submitted a plan for his consideration

that has proved extremely effective for countless individuals. I submit it here for you, for whether your faith is strong or weak, this is an exercise which I believe all of us could undertake with benefit once or twice a year.

Surround yourself as much as possible with believers; try to affiliate yourself with a prayer group; and attend healing services regularly, for here you will find yourself in an atmosphere of almost palpable faith. Then undertake what I call the thirty-day experiment of faith. For a period of one month act and live the promises of Jesus as if you believed with the unqualified fervency of the early Christians.

For thirty days, awaken each morning with His name on your lips. Before getting out of bed, offer Him praise and thanksgiving for another day, and offer Him your life for that day, praying that the Holy Spirit will guide you in all you do and say.

For thirty days, pray regularly, if only for a few minutes, morning, noon, and night, and throughout the day observe the presence of God by frequently offering brief sentence-prayers of praise.

For thirty days, read fifteen minutes a day of the New Testament, always asking first the guidance of the Holy Spirit. Read with special care of our Lord's healing miracles, as if you really *believed* that He is the same yesterday, today, and forever (He. 13:8). Read all of the First Epistle of Saint John each week. This is a short epistle, and so filled with the love of God that no one who reads it under the guidance of the Spirit can fail to respond.

Before going to sleep at night, ask the forgiveness of God for any sin you may have committed, and *believe* that you are forgiven. Finally, ask yourself whether you have done one thing that day because *He* said to do it, or whether that day you have abstained from one thing because He said *not* to do it. I suggest this final exercise for an important reason: It is a curious thing that while true faith leads to obedience, the converse is likewise true —obedience leads to a viable faith.

Live by the tiny light you have, which may be only your *desire* for faith in the Lord Jesus, and you will receive increasingly more. Cardinal Newman once said, "To all who wish for light, but cannot find it, one precept must be given: OBEY." I have seen the validity of these words confirmed again and again.

During this period of thirty days, you will probably be assaulted by such thoughts as, "This is silly. I don't need this; my faith is strong enough." Or, "This is ridiculous. I don't believe any of it." Whatever form these assaults take, praise God for them, for the closer you come to Him, the more violently Satan will assail you with such thoughts. Be firm with your "Get thee behind me, Satan," and continue on your way, unafraid to pray, "Lord, I believe; help thou mine unbelief." No matter how strong our faith, there are few of us who do not occasionally cry out to God with this prayer. God will honor it, as He did when the father of a sick boy spoke it nearly two thousand years ago (Mark 9:24). But, now as then, He still wants to hear those first words: "Lord, I believe."

At the end of the month, if your desire to believe wholly in Christ has been strong and sincere, you are virtually assured of finding yourself with an undaunted faith and the courage to claim His promises in your own life. He will honor your faith, and your life will be transfigured.

So it was with the man I mentioned earlier. At the end of the allotted thirty days, he found (somewhat to his own surprise) that he actually *did* believe with his heart those things that before he had said only with his lips. He still had his anxieties and apprehensions, but they had lessened and now he could cope with them. Today he is a truly committed Christian. His spiritual life is strong; his marriage has been restored by the love of Christ he now manifests; and his deep-seated emotional difficulties are a thing of the past. He has learned the verity of the words "This is the victory which overcometh the world, even our faith" (I John 5:4).

He is still not completely healed physically, although he is much improved. As he awaits the complete healing of his body, he says, "It no longer seems to really matter to me whether I am physically healed or not. What *does* matter are the things I now know: that Jesus is *my* Saviour; the reality of His love, and the fact that He is always with me." Such an attitude is always cause for rejoicing, for it indicates true wholeness—the kind that matters most—and it also goes a long way toward assuring physical healing.

This man continues to attend healing services, after asking so common a question that it is worth mentioning here.

"Isn't it a lack of faith," he wondered, "to continue to pray for healing after praying once and then committing oneself to God?"

The answer to this question is an emphatic "No." Our Lord's admonition is to pray persistently—and to faint not (Luke 18:1). Again and again He gives us parables to illustrate how God honors persevering prayer, such as the stories of the friend at midnight (Luke 11:5–8) and the importunate widow (Luke 18:1–8).

Persevering prayer, far from denoting lack of faith, is an act of obedience to our Lord. Coming to Him again and again in expectancy demonstrates not faltering, but rather an unshakable and unswerving faith in the goodness and mercy of God, who has assured us that "him that cometh to me I will in no wise cast out" (John 6:37).

This coming to God is repeatedly emphasized throughout the New Testament, and especially in the Lord's Prayer. Here we ask, "Give us this day our daily bread"; we don't pray once a year for a twelve months' supply. We cannot store up God's grace. He wants us to come to Him continually. We don't, for example, receive holy communion once in a lifetime, for we cannot bank the grace received. We partake of His Body and Blood again and again.

In the healing ministry we respond to His call, "Come unto Me," on a continuous and continuing basis. At first we may go a little hesitantly, not quite sure what is involved. Our courage increases, and each time, by the leading of the Spirit, we come a little closer to Him, until at last we come boldly unto the throne of grace (Heb. 4:16). Standing now on holy ground, we begin to understand the meaning of it all. To Him who has known us before the foundation of the world (Eph. 1:4, 5), we offer our entire beings, having recognized Him at long last. As we now call Him by name and prostrate ourselves in adoration at His feet, He extends His hand and blesses us, and we are made whole.

I believe it behooves us all to examine the true nature of faith. You have not real faith until you can say and mean it, "Though he slay me, yet will I put my trust in him" (Job 13:15). You have not real faith if you say, as I heard a minister say of a woman dying of cancer, "If she recovers, I'll believe in the power of God to heal." Faith is not dependent upon signs. You have not a real understanding of faith if, your own body touched by the healing Christ, you look at another who is not physically perfect and say, "If he had *my* faith, he would be healed." For as many unbelievers are healed (through the faith of others), so are many of the faithful physically unhealed, though never left untouched by His healing hand.

I think often of a religious conference I happened

to attend. At the conference was a little woman, crippled from birth, who had long ago committed her life to Christ. She attends healing services regularly, praying always for others, and that God will use her life for His glory.

I was greatly disturbed when at the conference I happened to overhear someone say to her, in a tone both condescending and arrogant, "If you really believed in God, you'd be healed. Look at *me*. I was healed because I had faith."

Later that night, the devout and holy little woman came to me in tears. "But I *do* believe in God," she said, "and I know He can heal. Does the fact that I limp mean there's something wrong with my faith?"

After talking with her for a while, we prayed together, and she left reassured. And that night I prayed fervently for the person who had made that remark. So much harm, so much unnecessary suffering, is caused by the ignorance and insensitivity of those who profess to be working in the name of Christ and witnessing for His sake.

Everyone who believes in the Lord Jesus is saved, but he is not always physically healed. We do not know why, but we are sure that the failure is not necessarily due to a personal lack of deep faith. We base our certainty not only on the teaching of the ancient church—which placed the responsibility for failure to heal on herself, as the Body—but also on the Scripture from which this teaching was derived. For although our Lord frequently said to the one healed, "Thy faith hath made thee whole," He also healed the multitudes, many of whom, it is safe to assume, did not hold an intense personal faith. To be sure, He made clear that faith *somewhere* is necessary, whether it be the faith of friends, of the group as a whole, or of the one who ministers. While we cannot ever underestimate the value of the faith of one who seeks healing, we must also note that Jesus did not always demand personal faith. He did not, for example, demand faith of Malchus, when He healed the ear of the servant of the high priest (Luke 22:50, 51), and it is highly unlikely that this man believed he would be healed.

Nor did Jesus mention the faith of the man with palsy brought to the Great Physician by his friends (Mark 2:3–5). So crowded was the house where Jesus was that the sick man's friends could not get him near our Lord, so they let down the bed of the invalid through the roof. We are told that when Jesus saw the faith of the sick man's *friends*, He said, "Son, thy sins are forgiven thee," and the man with palsy was healed. Jesus did not mention *his* faith (or lack of it), only the faith of his friends.

When persons come to me, as did a woman not long ago, saying, "Please help me achieve faith so I can be healed," I am given pause to think. In our too-often harassed and frenetic efforts to "achieve" faith, we are putting the cart before the horse. In a very real sense, it is Christ and not faith we should be seeking.

"I live now not with my own life but with the life of Christ who lives in me," says Saint Paul. Therefore it follows, as the apostle says, that "the life I now live in this body, I live in faith" (Gal. 2:20 Jer.). This means simply that if you are aware that Christ lives in you, you have all the faith you can possibly need, for Christ *is* your faith.

The ancient church sought Christ and Christ alone, and as a result great miracles followed. And so it is today: Miracles occur in direct proportion to the fervency with which we seek our Lord. *Your* miracle of healing will occur in one form or another if your quest is Christ for His sake, and not faith for faith's sake.

Chapter 11

PREPARING THE CLIMATE FOR HEALING

As WE ARE NEVER out of God's love, so are we never beyond the reach of His healing hand. He longs to restore us to wholeness; to heal our ailing bodies, our tormented minds, our alienated spirits, our broken relationships. In short, He yearns to heal us even more than we long to be healed.

Although we may not know why everyone is not healed, we do know something of the conditions which, generally speaking, must be met if we are to be made whole. We know the necessity of establishing and living in a spiritual climate which will best enable us to receive His healing power, and above all Himself.

It is perfectly true that during our Lord's earthly ministry He healed all who came to Him: "And great multitudes followed Him and He healed them all" (Matt. 12:15). It seems obvious that Jesus did not tell the people who followed Him that they had to establish a particular "climate" for healing. He simply saw their need, and He met it.

Why, then, you may wonder, do we emphasize the

necessity of such a climate today? Simply because we are living in an era of unparalleled unbelief that extends even into the church. We are assailed on all sides by the knowledge of men, which seeks to obscure the wisdom of God. We need a climate for healing not for God's sake, that He may then consent to make us whole, but for *our* sakes, that we may more readily receive that which He stands so ready to give.

To prepare such a climate we must first rid ourselves, with God's help, of those factors within ourselves which lock our hearts against Him. Asking the guidance of the Holy Spirit, we examine ourselves, seeking to find, to recognize, and to call by name, those sins that separate us from Him. We may well not be guilty of any overt sins, but we may find ourselves surprised at the resentments, jealousies, envy, feelings of hostility, and similar sins of the spirit that we are harboring—all of which set up a barrier to the inflow of Christ's life in our lives.

After a general preliminary examination of ourselves, which is the first step toward establishing the climate for healing, and after a brief daily self-examination (which should be limited to three or four minutes to avoid morbid introspection), it is enough to pray, "Search me, O God, and know my heart: try me and know my thoughts: and see if there be any wicked way in me" (Ps. 139:3, 4); "Wash me thoroughly from mine iniquity, and cleanse me from my sin" (Ps. 51:2).

Little by little those spiritual sins that may be separating us from God and hindering His healing power will be unearthed. The next step is to get rid of them, which is often far from easy.

In another book I have submitted some concrete suggestions in the form of certain symbolic acts accompanied by prayer, which have proved helpful to many.[1]

---

[1] Emily Gardiner Neal, *Where There's Smoke* (New York: Morehouse-Barlow, 1967), p. 151.

As one more example of such an act, I cite the recent experience of a young clergyman who wrote me in real distress, saying that for the first time in his life he felt not only resentment but actual hatred against a certain individual. He had prayed hard and long but apparently to no avail, and finally in desperation he had written to me for help. Before I had time to answer this letter, I received another, this time an exuberant one, telling me that he was now completely liberated from his destructive emotion.

He had devised his own "act." He had written a letter expressing all that he felt: the hostility, the hate, the anger. He had sealed the letter with Scotch tape and put it in the back of an unused drawer; he locked the drawer and then threw away the key. This was a symbolic gesture of "putting away" his hate. It was a sacramental act, an outward and visible sign of an inward and spiritual intention that the love of God fill him once again. It worked. The hate was gone, locked out of his life; the entire situation was overtaken by God's love.

No two people are alike, and no one method is helpful to all individuals. I remember well the woman who came to me announcing that she was going to leave her husband. She was filled with bitterness against the man to whom she had been married for twenty-five years. Their life together was filled with bickering, hostility, and general incompatibility. I talked with her many times and from the human point of view, the situation appeared hopeless. After praying each time we were together that Christ's love might overshadow this marriage and restore all brokenness, I told her that I would not see her again until she agreed to hold up her husband each day in the love of Christ, asking God to bless him, asking forgiveness for her inability to love (however justified this inability might seem), and praying that God would enable her to love as He did.

One day, about three months later, she came to me and with wonderment in her voice said, "You know, I prayed as you told me for a long time. Then suddenly one day I realized I hadn't prayed that way for weeks. I realized that it wasn't because I had *forgotten*, but that it was no longer necessary. God had answered me, and I had come at last to really love my husband."

The next week she attended a healing service to offer thanksgiving for her happy marriage.

One of the vital conditions for healing in every area of our lives consists of forgiveness: the forgiveness of God toward us and our forgiveness toward those who have wronged us—or those whom we *think* have wronged us, which as far as we are concerned, amounts to the same thing. "Forgive us our trespasses as we forgive those who trespass against us." Unless we forgive others, God cannot forgive us, for unless we have first forgiven, we have within us a wall of bitterness and resentment that closes us off from God. If we are to receive Him and His healing grace, we must become open channels through which His power can flow—and lack of forgiveness on our parts clogs that channel with particles of resentment, or envy or hate or self-pity. These constitute the cholesterol of the soul. The dissolvent for this spiritual cholesterol is forgiveness.

"Forgive us our trespasses as we forgive those who trespass against us." These words tended to puzzle me years ago. They seemed to imply the attitude, "All right, Lord. See how magnanimous I am to forgive so-and-so. Therefore You must now forgive me."

One day I realized that the whole basis of forgiveness is love, and what this phrase from the Lord's Prayer really meant was: "We know Your forgiveness, Lord. Please help us to forgive like that."

As in our relationship with God *He* was the first to love—"We love God because He first loved us" (I John

4:19)—so likewise He was the first to forgive: He died on the cross for our sins. So although we must forgive others if God is to be able to forgive us, yet it is God who has performed the first and great act of forgiveness. It is through Him, and by His grace alone, that we are enabled to forgive.

The best way I know to help us forgive those who have trespassed against us is to think of what Christ has done for us. If we fail to accept in our hearts the fact that we are pardoned sinners, if we fail to live in the knowledge of God's merciful forgiveness, we ourselves cannot possibly forgive.

Once having learned to forgive, and by God's grace gotten rid of those factors that hinder His healing power in our lives, the soil for healing is prepared. But there are still conditions to be met before the climate is established.

There is, for example, that attitude of thanksgiving which is an essential element of the healing climate. It is easy enough to be thankful when all goes well, but perhaps we cannot know the full meaning of thanksgiving until things have gone badly. In my own experience it has been within the context of pain that I have learned best how to be truly thankful—and for such prosaic things as I had always before taken for granted.

For over two and a half years, for example, I was unable to sit upright with my legs outstretched. This meant that I could not take a hot bath, and anyone with a bad back knows the relief afforded by a tub of hot water. The first time I was able to lower myself into a bathtub still stands out in my memory as a momentous event, and I have never forgotten my inexpressible gratitude to God. Every single day since that memorable occasion, as I step into a hot bath I fervently thank God that I am able to do so. Such a small thing, but for me it was, and still is, a minor miracle!

No matter how bad things may be, we can always

find something to be thankful for. The continual offering of our thanksgiving for things great and small becomes habitual with practice. When it becomes habitual, we have established an attitude indispensable to healing, whether of mind, body, or spirit.

Then there is the matter of obedience, which, like love, is an indispensable element in the climate of healing. It is obedience that leads us to the kingdom, obedience that springs from love. It is out of love—the love we bear for Christ—that we are constrained to obey. "If a man love me, he will keep my words," our Lord says (John 14:23).

We obey His words not out of fear, not for any reward that we think may result, but purely and simply out of love. As Saint Peter says, we ought to obey God rather than man, and the Holy Ghost is given to them that obey Him (Acts 5:29, 32). As the Holy Spirit is God active in our lives, without Him we are utterly helpless, without strength or life.

Whether or not we *understand* why He commands us to do certain things matters not at all. What *does* matter is that we do what He tells us to do. "Whatsoever he saith unto you, do it," said the Virgin Mary (John 2: 5). She was a perfect example of human obedience, which it behooves us all to follow.

The task of any Christian is simply to obey the divine command. His comfort, His strength, His healing, are always there, but our reception of them is dependent upon His grace, which He liberally bestows upon His obedient servants. Obedience is the cost of receiving in our lives that gift without price—something of the power of the living God. It is the cost if we are to receive the greatest of all blessings, an experiential knowledge of the risen, healing Christ.

Finally, I would mention trust, which is the other side of the coin of faith, and an intrinsic part of a total faith.

For it is quite possible to have a dynamic faith in God and still lack that quiet trust in Him which is essential to the healing climate.

To the precise extent that we trust Him we are enabled to live in His peace, without fear for today or apprehension for the future. "Thou wilt keep him in perfect peace, whose mind is stayed on Thee; because he trusteth in Thee" (Isa. 26:3). Self-reliance is considered a highly commendable virtue in our culture, but unless we are willing to substitute God-dependence for self-reliance, we can never claim this promise, nor can we ever know the meaning of true security. Until we learn to put our complete trust in Him, we will never comprehend His words, "My own peace I give you, a peace the world cannot give" (John 14:27); and failing to understand, we will be unable to appropriate one of His greatest gifts.

Many inquire about the need and method of preparation before attending a specific healing service. In my experience, there is great need for spiritual preparation before the service as well as during the service itself, which by including prayers of praise, thanksgiving, confession, and Scripture reading is a corporate reaffirmation of that preparation which has gone before. Whether one is attending a healing mission or regular weekly healing services, the preparation is ideally the same.

First comes fasting, which I believe to be invaluable. To do without food quickens the spirit, making the individual more receptive to the power of God (or if he is attending a service as intercessor, a more open channel for His healing grace). When the disciples asked Jesus why they had been unable to cast out an evil spirit, He replied, "This kind can come forth by nothing, but by prayer and fasting" (Mark 9:29). And so it seems today with many illnesses.

Prepare yourself before the service by much prayer,

predominantly of praise and thanksgiving. Examine your conscience and ask forgiveness for anything amiss in your life. Read Scripture, especially the accounts of some of the healing miracles. If time allows, do some spiritual reading. Attempt, in so far as you are able, to live those hours before the healing service in the spirit, in an attitude of prayer and meditation.

As more supplicants have learned the value of this prior preparation, the healing power of God has been increasingly manifested; this in turn has increased the faith of the church.

Chapter 12

LIVING IN
THE CLIMATE

HAVING PREPARED THE CLIMATE FOR HEALING, the next step is learning to live in that climate. It is the same atmosphere, actually, in which all who call themselves Christians might well endeavor to live, for "were you not taught the truth as it is in Jesus? You must be made new in mind and spirit, and put on the new nature of God's creating, which shows itself in the just and devout life" (Eph. 4:20–24 N.E.B.).

This "just and devout life," which is the Christian way as well as the climate for healing, is characterized by love and joy and peace, by praise and thanksgiving. To live in this way is *being* a Christian, with His life in you. This means not merely trying to follow Christ, it means to belong to Him with your entire self, body, mind, and spirit. To be such a Christian (not solely to attempt to live as one) means complete joy, a joy that permeates to the innermost depths of our being.

To be a Christian does not mean that we shall never

know pain or trouble or sickness. It does mean that we need never suffer from complete despair. For we know it is as Saint Paul says: Nothing can ever separate us from the love of God, and in all things, tribulation and distress, persecution and peril, we are more than conquerors through Him that loves us (Rom. 8:35).

Are these just pious words? I used to think so, and I remember how irritably I had said before I became a Christian, "It's just plain stupid to expect anyone to be joyous or thankful if he is sick or in pain or bereaved."

I have thought of that remark many times over the past years, when events in my own life gave them the lie. I recently thought of it again when an old friend who is still an agnostic said to me, "Are you honestly happier now as a Christian?"

My reply was a spontaneous "Of course! I never knew before what real joy was."

That I could make such a response seems to me a miracle in itself; for even as I spoke, there flashed through my mind the things that have happened to me since I embraced the faith. I felt once again, as I feel it so often, that welling up of thanksgiving that when these things *had* happened, I had *been* a Christian—for without Christ I would have been destroyed.

The more of God we are able to receive, the greater our wholeness, for in Him we possess those elements that comprise the climate of healing: an ever-increasing love and joy; the growing desire to praise and worship; the greatful heart that in time habitually offers thanksgiving regardless of outward circumstances.

These factors are the involuntary result of the risen Christ in our lives; at the same time, they constitute the spiritual laws that most of us break again and again. With most of us it is as Saint Paul says: "For what I would, that do I not; but what I hate, that do I" (Rom. 7:15).

I recall all too vividly how one night at dinner my husband and I were discussing someone who had done a grave injustice to one of our children.

"I hate her so much I could kill her!" I burst out.

Later that night, when alone in the house, ironing, I seemed actually to hear the words, so strongly were they impressed upon my heart: "Whosoever looketh on a woman to lust after her hath committed adultery with her already in his heart" (Matt. 5:28).

I remembered then what I had said at the dinner table. Not only had I broken the law of love, but I had broken the sixth commandment, for I had committed murder in my heart. Not even stopping to set the iron upright, I dropped to my knees and offered Him my contrite spirit. I still remember, years later, the healing of God's absolving grace as it washed over me. And I still have the scorched pillow case I was ironing at the time, to serve as a reminder.

As Saint Paul says, we all sin and we all break at one time or another one or more of the spiritual laws of healing, thus polluting the climate in which we are trying to live. But God stands always ready in His never-failing mercy to forgive and restore us, so the atmosphere in which we strive to live is cleansed and purified once more.

The perfect climate of healing, which few of us can attain but which it is our holy obligation continually to attempt to create and then live in, requires the most difficult of all things for most of us: the death of self. This final act is one that our Lord demands of all who make an effort to follow Him.

"If any man will come after me," He says, "let him deny himself, and take up his cross and follow me" (Matt. 16:24).

Jesus did not mean by "denying" oneself to give up

some material pleasure one might desire; He meant that we must renounce ourselves. This renunciation of self is a continual struggle, but a joyful one, in which we engage purely out of the love we bear for Him to Whom we offer our lives; it is a battle whose victory lies in unconditional surrender. It means the alignment of our wills with His, so that there are not two wills—His and ours—but one will: His.

It means a daily (perhaps hourly) "funeral" of self; but it is a "white" funeral and therefore a gloriously triumphant one. We know that only when we are dead to self can we be empty of self and thus be filled by God.

There are probably few of us who work publicly in the healing ministry who have not been told from time to time by people in the congregation that as we were speaking, there was visible above our heads a nimbus, a circle of radiant light. Some time ago a phenomenon was reported to me that I treasure above all else that has happened during a healing service, for from it I learned so invaluable a lesson.

It was the final service of a very strenuous mission, and by the time that last service came, I was exhausted and my back so painful that I wondered how I could ever get through it. Just before it was time to speak, I remember praying, "Lord, take from me all desire except that Thy most holy will may be done this night. Empty me of self, and fill me with Thyself. This time, Lord, please speak not only *through* me but *for* me."

As I stepped into the pulpit, I was conscious of a surge of supernatural strength; and as I spoke, I experienced His anointing in a totally new and wonderful way.

After the service, someone drew me aside and said, "Tonight as you were speaking, the most extraordinary thing happened. I was looking at you and you suddenly disappeared. I could hear your voice, but in the pulpit there was only a brilliant light where you had been standing."

I was grateful for this, but attributed it to a purely subjective experience on this person's part. However, within ten days I received three letters, two of them from clergymen and all of them from "down-to-earth" people, reporting the same phenomenon. I could then only rejoice at His answer to prayer.

"Give thanks for all things" is the scriptural admonition (Eph. 5:20). This must, then, include adversity, which is a challenge enabling us to prove our faith; grief, for it cleanses and throws us completely on the mercy of God, Who binds up the wounds of the broken-hearted (Isa. 61:1); and pain, for God will use it for His glory to alleviate the pain of others. In everything give thanks, adjures Saint Paul. And I know now that this is possible for Christians, for we neither suffer nor sorrow as those who have no hope (I Thess. 4:13).

Hitherto I had given thanks for the way in which God had used my pain, and for the relief of pain, however brief, when it had come. Now, for the first time, I was able to thank Him for the suffering itself; for had I not been in such pain that night of the mission, I doubt that I could have prayed with such wholehearted fervency that He empty me completely of self. There was great healing in this experience; for a short time at least, the climate was as He would have it to be.

To establish the right climate for healing is not easy. To attempt to live one's life in such a climate is even more difficult—but it is a glorious striving, whose goal is God Himself. For in direct proportion to the extent that we are able, by His grace, to relinquish ourselves, to that extent are we able to receive Him who is at once the Light that shineth in our darkness (John 1:5), the source of all joy, of all health and wholeness, and not only the meaning of our life, but life itself.

Chapter 13

LORD, HEAR OUR PRAYER

ACCORDING TO SAINT TERESA of Avila, "There is but one road which reaches God, and that is prayer."

This is, of course, true, but prayer is not only the road to God. It constitutes the very atmosphere we breathe in the climate of healing; it is the oxygen of the spirit. It is the means by which we establish a relationship with God, and the means through which we are enabled to live continually in that relationship.

As we constantly caution that there is no magic in the sacramental healing rites, so must this caution be extended to prayer, and particularly to healing prayer, for there is no magical formula that inevitably results in healing.

There are many ways of private prayer, and no two people pray in precisely the same way. This is not to say that how we pray is not extremely important; it is. But the importance lies not so much in the words we say as in the attitude behind them. I see a danger, especially in the healing ministry, that because the technique of healing prayer is emphasized, the methodology for some people may supersede the underlying attitude.

For example, we teach that in praying for the sick, we must erase from our minds the symptoms of illness and picture the patient as completely whole. There is great validity in this, but to overemphasize this procedure is to run the risk of thinking that there is some sort of magic involved, that if one's prayer is not accompanied by a vision of the individual as totally well, no healing can possibly result. Although experience indicates that certain kinds of healing prayer are more effective than others, to attempt to stereotype such prayer, to insist that one must pray at all times in exactly the same way, may well lead to superstition.

In praying for healing, we recommend affirmative prayer, not using the escape clause *"If* it be Thy will." Assuming that perfect wholeness *is* God's will, we can pray with assurance; "Thy will be done in him for whom I pray." We suggest offering thanks for the healing even before it is evident; we ask the patient to act, insofar as possible, as if the healing had already taken place. This does not mean stopping medication or throwing away braces. It simply means to adopt an attitude of health, attempting to live a normal life. Insistence upon these methods as invariable and inflexible techniques, however, may carry with it the connotation of magic. In my opinion the elements of prayer we must insist upon as indispensable are those that reflect an attitude of praise and thanksgiving, not only for the healing that has already been begun but also for the privilege of being able to take *everything* to God. "In every thing by prayer and supplication with thanksgiving, let your requests be made known unto God," says Saint Paul (Phil. 4:6).

Scripture tells us that Christ lives to make intercession for us (Heb. 7:25). Thus if we begin our prayers with the supplication "Pray Thyself in me," we cannot go wrong, and there will be no danger of perverting our prayer of the heart into magic incantations of unfelt words.

One of the first requisites of prayer is an inner quiet, a willingness "to be still and know that I am God" (Ps. 46:10). The restlessness of the age in which we live, the frantic running from one religious conference to another, the desire to dwell continuously on the mountain tops of religious experience, are unhealthy. In order truly to pray, it helps to begin by realizing that prayer is not a flamboyant experience to be always ecstatically enjoyed but a quiet relationship with God which is total joy.

The words we say may differ, but there is a general pattern to be followed if we are to pray as Christians. In all prayer, for example, we offer God ourselves. We offer Him our love, praying that He intensify it. We offer Him our faith, praying that He quicken it. We offer Him our commitment, praying that He increase it. We pray that He will cleanse us and use our lives for His glory.

In prayer for healing there is an inevitable tension between battling the evil of sickness and suffering and simultaneously relinquishing ourself, or the one for whom we pray, entirely to God. The value of the words we say lies in the fact that they clarify our thoughts and thus our attitude, an attitude that may be expressed in words something like this: "Take my life, O Lord. Transform it and use it for the blessing [healing] of John Smith."

Believing that it is God's perfect will that we be healed of all brokenness, we know also that the most important healing, and our only real wholeness, lies in offering ourselves to Him that He may fill us with His spirit.

There are many ways of praying for the sick, some of which I have mentioned in another book.[1] Suffice it to say here that among the most simple and effective is that

[1] Emily Gardiner Neal, *Where There's Smoke* (New York: Morehouse-Barlow, 1967), p. 157.

of holding up in the healing light and love of Christ each one for whom we pray. As we take them one by one before the throne of grace, we express our attitude of confidence and trust in those words voiced so long ago: "Lord, behold, he whom thou lovest is sick" (John 11:3). In these words of Martha and Mary, Saint Augustine finds what he terms a model of prayer, teaching us to have immediate recourse to God without waiting until all human means of aid have been exhausted.[2] I myself have found it one of the most powerful of prayers, reflecting our conviction of God's infinite mercy and never-failing compassion.

If we are in doubt, we can never go wrong if we use the prayer our Lord gave us: "Thy will be done on earth as it is in heaven." This one sentence conveys the underlying attitude of all healing prayer as for our entire Christian life.

The story is told of a Franciscan friar of some years ago that everyone he prayed for seemed to recover. Soon people began to come to him from many miles away, as though to a shrine. Again and again his superior asked him about his power, and he invariably replied, "*I* have no power; *I* do nothing. It is God."

Finally the superior learned from him how he prayed.

"I pray only one prayer," the friar said: " 'Thy will be done on earth as it is in heaven.' And I pray it one hundred times each night and morning." Perhaps this is the only prayer any of us would need to pray if we prayed it with all our hearts.

In my experience, the prayer of pure praise also releases exceptional healing power. At least part of the power of this prayer can surely be attributed to the fact that it is entirely selfless.

Many are confused by the distinction made between

[2] A Father of the Society of Jesus, *Practical Meditations* (London: Burns and Oates, 1962), p. 717.

praise and thanksgiving. As one woman put it, "You seem to be quibbling over words." No—for while thanksgiving and praise go hand in hand, the difference is not merely a matter of semantics; it lies in a subtle but important difference in attitude. In thanksgiving, as in the other essentials of Christian prayer, all of which are necessary to our total prayer life, there is a strong element of self. In confession, for example, we are thinking of *our* sins; in intercession we are praying for those for whom *we* seek God's blessing; in petition we are asking His help for *our* needs. Likewise, in thanksgiving we are thanking God for something which in some way pleases *us*. However, in the prayer of pure praise, there is no element of self, only simple adoration, and for this reason praise brings us extraordinarily close to God. It might be remarked here that God has not an insatiable craving for our adoration. He needs neither us nor our continual praise. We need *Him*, and the attitude of praise on our parts is for our benefit, and not His.

The well-known novelist Elizabeth Goudge has a priest in one of her books comment that there are three vitally important prayers, each consisting of only three words: "Thee I adore," "Christ have mercy," and "Into Thy hands." Upon these brief prayers we might well build our entire prayer lives, for they convey the attitudes which should lie behind all the prayers we say, in whatever words we choose to use.

During the past few years, much emphasis has been placed on conversational prayer, and rightly so; without such prayer one cannot, in my opinion, be said to truly pray. Yet it is curious that this method of prayer is considered "new," for it has been used for many centuries, as the lives of the great saints of the church attest. Indeed, the classical "textbook" on conversational prayer, Brother Lawrence's *The Practice of the Presence of God*, dates from the seventeenth century.

Typical is the story told of Saint Teresa of Avila, who, when on an unusually arduous journey, complained to God of the difficulties He was placing in her way. When He seemed to reply, "But that is how I treat My friends," the saint answered irritably, "Yes, my Lord, and that is why Thou hast so few of them." [3] This is an amusing and valid example of conversational prayer, in which one talks to God as one feels.

Genuine prayer does not put on pious airs or engage in pietistic rhetoric. We talk to God naturally, telling Him how and what we feel: of our victories and disappointments; of our desires for others and for ourselves; of our gratitude and of our love. Again, this is for *our* benefit, not His. Our talking with Him establishes that personal relationship upon which depends the strength of our prayer life.

Any conversation is a two-way affair, and at least half our prayer time should be spent in listening. Jesus says, "If any man will do His will, he shall know of the doctrine" (John 7:17), which is to say that the insight and knowledge concerning what He taught, the ability to discern the truth that He not only represented but was and is, are given those who do His will.

Many of us fervently desire to be obedient to Him in the specific circumstances in which we find ourselves. The question is, how do we *know* His will in any given situation?

As necessary and good as is Christian vocal prayer, listening prayer is absolutely essential for our spiritual growth, which necessarily includes obedience. For it is only when we listen that we can hear Him speak; and in the noisy activism of the world, that still small voice needs quiet of heart and mind if it is to be heard. With practice we will be able to hear it. Usually the voice

[3] E. Allison Peers, *Mother of Carmel* (London: S.C.M. Press, 1945), p. 136.

comes not as a sound, but as a sense of deep, abiding peace, or a strong, unmistakable impression of what our course of action should be if it is to be according to God's will.

While none of us prays in exactly the same way, I submit one method by which you may learn the art of listening prayer.

First, as in all your prayers, ask that the Holy Spirit pray in you. Say whatever words you wish, but let your attitude be, "Speak, Lord, for thy servant heareth" (I Sam. 3:9). And then be quiet.

I think it useful, especially in the beginning when you are learning to listen, to focus your eyes on something, a cross or a crucifix, or perhaps a picture of Christ. If you close your eyes, it is fatally easy for your thoughts to wander. Even so, from time to time you will find yourself distracted. At these times, draw yourself back by silently repeating the holy name. This is not "vain repetition," for each time you say "Jesus" it is with a different emphasis: "I worship You"; "Have mercy"; "Forgive"; "Open my ears that I may hear Your voice." Speak the holy name slowly, with long intervals of silence in between. It is in these times of silence that you will finally hear.

In so praying, you may be led into contemplation, to which one comes by the prayer of simplicity and quiet. The word "contemplation" need not frighten you. It means in essence and in its simplest form just being with God in love; your mind, your lips, and even your heart stilled, your spirit fixed on God. This type of prayer is not for a favored few living the enclosed life, It is, as the Archbishop of Canterbury writes, "accessible to any man, woman or child who is ready to try to be obedient and humble, and to want God very much." [4] As the Archbishop

[4] Arthur Michael Ramsey, *Sacred and Secular* (New York: Harper and Row, 1965), p. 45.

goes on to say, "Contemplative prayer is the prayer of hunger and thirst, of desire for God—such is the prayer which links Christianity and ordinary life." [5]

No matter how you choose to go about it, it is necessary, if you would be obedient, not only to scan Scripture seeking to obey the injunctions of our Lord found there, but to search the mind of Christ, which can be done only by the spirit of God within you. It is He who reveals that which we must know in order to be truly obedient, and in our obedience, enabled by grace to comprehend, however inadequately, God's revelation of Himself; to have, by the action of the Holy Spirit, God's will illumined for us.

The goal of the Christian is to live in a state of habitual prayer, to which we come by practicing the presence of God.

This we may do in a number of ways, no matter how busy we may be with other things. Brief words of praise may be offered throughout the day (as mentioned in Chapter 10); a "for Thy glory, Lord" spoken before each task we do; the frequent repetition of the holy name—any method you wish that will keep you aware of God.

The time will come, no matter how occupied our conscious minds, when our subconscious will be continually aware of Him. It will become a natural instinct and not a self-conscious effort to pray for those we pass on the street who look harassed or unhappy; to offer prayer as an ambulance clangs by or we pass a funeral procession.

Instinctively we will pray for the disagreeable taxi driver, and suddenly he smiles and begins to talk—and we know why. Instinctively we pray for the cross clerk in a store, and suddenly she becomes pleasant and cooperative. These are small miracles of prayer, but miracles they are. Countless people whom we shall never

[5] *Ibid.,* p. 58.

know may well be touched and blessed by our prayers in passing.

As Christians, we are called to pray for our enemies. I still remember the shock and indignation of some, when at the healing service at Calvary immediately following the assassination of Robert Kennedy, I offered prayer not only for the Kennedy family but for the assassin. "Bless them that curse you, and pray for them which despitefully use you, and persecute you" (Matt. 5:44) is His command.

Thus we pray as well for those we simply may not like. In our prayers we *will* them all the best; we *will* to love them, and often the time comes when we, through God, can even like them!

Our prayer life is not complete unless we set aside definite times for prayer, at least at night and in the morning. Some time ago, a woman who is under my spiritual direction demurred at the thought of any formal prayer time.

"I pray throughout the day," she said, "when I'm cleaning or washing the dishes or making the beds. Why then must I pray also at set times?"

Simply because there should be occasions when we go before the throne of almighty God giving Him our complete and undivided attention, the only thought on our minds Him whom we worship. We attempt to follow the example of our Lord, who, although His whole life was a prayer, yet withdrew again and again to pray.

If we practice the presence of God throughout the day, and if we draw apart, however briefly, at certain set intervals, prayer can become for us a way of life. Busy young parents can achieve this life as well as any monastic, and I know many who do.

It has been observed that many people, concerned solely with personal salvation, do not have a real sense of what the Body of Christ—of which we are all members and Christ the Head—really is. The importance of the corporate nature of the Body often seems to be underestimated.

Participating together in the worship of the church, we link our prayers with the faithful, with "angels and archangels and all the company of heaven" (B.C.P., p. 77). We are an indispensable part of a holy fellowship, spiritually one with all Christians, living and dead. To the extent that we fail to participate in corporate worship, to that extent do we weaken the Body.

There are many great liturgical prayers that we can make our own. These may help us develop in the life of prayer, so that we may outgrow the kindergarten prayers and attitudes of our childhood.

It behooves us to learn all we can about prayer, although we can never learn it all. Yet I think we must guard against becoming enmeshed in techniques. No "computerized" type of prayer, no matter how eloquent the words, can equal the silent lifting of the heart to God. I believe that no prayer, however inadequate (and all prayer is in some sense inadequate), goes unheard by Him—for it is as someone has said: "When a little girl prays for her rag doll, the whole world benefits." 6

6 *The Living Church*, Nov. 22, 1970, p. 2.

Chapter 14

DEPRESSION AND GUILT

SINCE I HAVE BEEN ASSOCIATED with the healing ministry, I have been confronted with an increasing number of cases of depression. These range from recurring bouts of feeling "down" to that deep depression which is devastating and in large part incapacitating.

Some cases of profound, long-lasting depression have been healed instantly by the power of God. Still more have been healed in a relatively short time by spiritual counseling and regular attendance at healing services. Others require the help of a psychologist or psychiatrist as well as healing prayer. If you are among the last, it is nothing to be ashamed of, any more than you should be ashamed of seeking medical help for a case of pneumonia. Both are illnesses, and if you require psychotherapy it does not denote a lack of faith. God can indeed heal all things. His power is always there for you to receive, but sometimes the very nature of your illness prevents your receiving it. Your heart is temporarily locked shut by the key of fear, which is symptomatic of emotional disturbance. A combination of prayer and psychiatric help will alleviate your fear, and as your tension lessens, your heart will open so that you may receive the healing grace God is so eager to bestow upon you.

To be forewarned is to be forearmed, and it is well to remember that if physical illness tends to be accompanied by guilt feelings, these feelings are often intensified in cases of depression. We think that as Christians who know and believe the incredibly good news of the gospel, we should never feel "down," but instead continually manifest in our lives the joy of the Lord. So we should, when we are well; but sometimes we cannot when we are emotionally disturbed. It is a curious paradox that the Christian, who of all people knows the source of all forgiveness, should at the same time suffer so greatly from feelings of guilt. This must continually break the heart of God, for it actually negates our Lord's sacrifice on the cross for our sins.

Not long ago I received a letter from a clergyman who lives far from Pittsburgh. It was a heartbreaking letter, telling me of his battle against a depression from which he could not extricate himself and which had completely incapacitated him as far as his work was concerned. Adding to the difficulty of the entire situation was the fact that his teen-age children were disillusioned and their faith seriously undermined.

"How," they asked "could it be possible that their father, a dedicated Christian minister, could be so afflicted?" Such questioning in the face of illness, disaster, or death is the reason I so continually emphasize that Christianity is not a passport into a utopian land of no disease, no trouble of any kind. What *is* unique to the Christian is his knowledge that the trials and tribulations of this world have no dominion over him, that the promise "He will not fail thee nor forsake thee" (Deut. 31:6) is a valid one, that in this knowledge lies the Christian's strength and consolation.

The guilt feelings from which this pastor suffered were

insupportable, obviously intensified in him because of his calling. By his letter it was abundantly clear that this minister was seriously ill emotionally and should be receiving psychiatric help. However, on the spiritual side, I felt I could justifiably offer the counsel he sought. He was, for example, in such a state of despair that he was convinced that he was no longer within the providence of God. I could assure him, because I was so sure, that he was *not* outside God's grace, and that his only real sin lay in thinking his sins so great and his faith so small that God would not and could not forgive him.

I recalled to this tortured man, and asked him to claim, the scriptural promise: "If we confess our sins, He is faithful and just to forgive us our sins and to cleanse us from all unrighteousness" (I John 1:9). Then I suggested that he offer his doubts, his sins and his depression, to God. I related to him a story of which I am very fond, which is applicable not only to the distraught clergyman of whom I speak but also to every single one of us.

It concerns the desert father who offered to God his life of hardship, but God rejected it. Then the saint offered all his work in his translation of Holy Scripture— but God rejected this. Finally, in desperation, the desert father cried, "But Lord, I have offered You all I have. What then do You want?"

Loud and clear came the answer: "I want your sins, my son."

Our sins, our fears and doubts, are part of us. Our self-offering is not complete unless we also offer these. God wants all of us, *especially* our sins, that He may have the joy of forgiving.

For innumerable people, the prayer for the healing of the memories described by Agnes Sanford [1] and now

---

[1] Agnes Sanford, *Healing Gifts of the Spirit* (Philadelphia: J. B. Lippincott, 1966), p. 125.

used by many has proved extraordinarily effective. In brief, this prayer consists of taking the person in need to Jesus and asking Him to walk back through time, beginning with the person's infancy and continuing up to the present. Adapted to individual circumstances, my abbreviated version goes something like this: "Jesus, please go back in time to when this individual was a tiny baby crying for his bottle and feeling forsaken. Hold him in Your arms, Lord, and comfort him. Now please go to the bedside of this five-year-old child, who lies in his nursery afraid of the dark. Reach out Your hand, Lord, and comfort him, that he will not be afraid. Now please go to that ten-year-old who feels himself unjustly punished and rejected. Hold him, Lord, that he may know how greatly he is loved."

We continue in this vein through adolescence up to the present, asking at each stage of the patient's life that God will cleanse and forgive. We pray for the complete healing of all those early memories and impressions, offering thanksgiving at each stage, and ask that he be enabled by grace to receive the fullness of God's mercy and forgiveness won for us on Calvary.

A deeply devout woman who was suffering from depression used this prayer and, like so many, was delivered from her disturbance. At this writing there has been no recurrence for four years. She made one visit to her psychiatrist to present herself as healed. When she told him of this type of prayer, he was intensely interested, considered it excellent therapy, and asked her for a copy.

Some months ago a man wrote me from another state telling me that he was flying to Calvary for the healing service the following week. He asked to talk with me a few minutes before the service. The gentleman was suffering from deep depression and unable to work. Midway during our interview, he remarked that he was a physician, but had come to Calvary not as a doctor but as a Christian. When it was time to go in to the service, I asked him what his medical specialty was, and he replied that he was a psychiatrist.

At the healing service he came to me for the laying on of hands, and I prayed very briefly for the healing of the memories. After the service we met, and he told me of an extraordinary happening which had occurred at the altar rail. He said that as he received the laying on of hands with prayer, there suddenly flooded to the surface of his mind memories of anger, hostility, and feelings of rejection that he had undergone as a child; he had never known until that moment that they existed in his unconscious mind. As Jesus walked back through time in the life of this man, each hurt had been healed. A letter from him shortly thereafter told me he was back at work full time—a new creature in Christ.

If you are suffering from an inexplicable depression, you may well find this type of prayer beneficial. Ask someone to pray it for you, or pray it for yourself.

As depression is complicated by feelings of guilt, so can guilt lead to and increase depression. My personal observation leads me to conclude that generally speaking, people fall into three categories in their response to guilt.

First, there are those with strong guilt feelings who seek to deny their guilt, when actually there may be good reason for it. Real guilt cannot be stifled without deleterious consequences. A visit to Bellevue Hospital in New York made it clear that such guilt must be removed before the sick person can recover. This is why the cooperation of psychiatrist and clergyman is vitally important in the treatment of those who need to know the forgiveness of God before they can be successfully treated medically. In some cases, the ability to accept His forgiveness is of itself sufficent "treatment."

In this connection I recall a woman suffering from deep

depression deriving from guilt occasioned by a love affair in which she had engaged several years before she was married. Her psychiatrist had urged her to tell her husband of the affair, but before doing so, she consulted me. While trying never to interfere with the work of a psychiatrist, in this case I felt obliged to say that I thought this would be a great mistake; that she might well jeopardize her marriage, and that by the hurt inflicted thus upon her husband, her own sense of guilt would, in my opinion, be increased rather than diminished.

I remember how the despair in her eyes turned to hope, as with all the authority at my command, I assured her of the forgiveness of God. I recall how the hope in her eyes turned to joy, as holding her hands in mine, she repeated after me, "Jesus, I accept your forgiveness according to Your promise. Thank You." By so simple an act, that woman's burden of guilt lifted, and with it the depression, and her life was transformed.

In the second category of guilt are Christians who are overscrupulous in regard to their own soul-searching for possible and often nonexistent sins.

Scrupulosity is one of the bugbears many of us have to face as we grow in the spiritual life; for as we grow, we become increasingly aware of our own sin, which in the presence of the utter holiness of God appalls us. Up to a point, this is as it should be, for "He who says he is without sin deceives himself; and there is no truth in him" (I John 1:8). However, if we focus our attention exclusively on our sin instead of Christ, forgetting the mercy of God, if we attribute to ourselves sins of which we are not guilty, and agonize over sins of which we know we are, we become neurotically introverted. We have forgotten that while Saint John tells us that there is no truth in us if we say we are without sin, so does he tell us, in the very next verse, that "God is faithful and just to forgive us our sins." If we fail to progress to this latter pronouncement and do not accept the assurance of God's forgiveness, we do violence to the Christian faith.

In the third category of guilt are those who, if they have not committed an overt act, such as robbing a bank, honestly do not know what sin is; yet they feel guilty. Perhaps it is as some theologians have conjectured, that the guilt feelings which plague so many, Christians or not, stem from original sin.

There are various sins of the spirit of which most of us are guilty, at least from time to time—sins which wreak havoc in our lives. Here I want to mention specifically anger, because there is so much confusion about this emotion. Time and again I am asked if anger is ever justified. I believe that it is, and my belief is scripturally founded. But we must constantly beware of holding anger in hate, and attempting to justify such anger as "righteous indignation." To be angry in hate is obviously a sin; but there can be anger *without* sin, if on the other side of the coin is love.

Paul says, "Be angry and sin not" (Eph. 4:26). The Phillips translation reads, "Be sure your anger is not out of wounded pride or bad temper." Thus the source of our anger must be our guideline.

We recall the life of our Lord. He was a far cry from the namby-pamby, sentimental "sweet Jesus" of the old Sunday School books. Rather was He a virile man of power. He was gentle, yes, for gentleness and strength go hand in hand; it is only the strong who dare to be gentle.

Our Lord certainly manifested anger, but it was a holy anger, springing from love and concern. He drove out the money changers in the Temple (Matt. 21:12); "Ye generation of vipers," He exclaimed to the Pharisees (Matt. 12:34); and in no uncertain terms He hurled at them the words, "Woe unto you, scribes and Pharisees, hypocrites!" (Matt. 23:13). And when His disciples failed to heal the lunatic child, his response was "O faithless and perverse generation! How long shall I be with you? How long shall I suffer you!" (Matt. 17:17).

Such words surely denote anger. Nevertheless, His anger was always the other side of the coin of love. As we strive to follow in His footsteps, we, too, must realize that were it not for anger (*not* bad temper), were it not for righteous indignation, nothing constructive would ever be accomplished in the world, no injustice ever rectified, no bad laws ever changed to good.

The opposite of righteous indignation may well be indifference—for indifference, not anger, is to me the sin of the world. It is indifference, not atheism, that is the arch enemy of the Christian faith; and where there is indifference, there is no concern for minority groups, for the poor, for all who suffer.

"Be angry and sin not." But let us be angry over situations and not at people. This is another way of saying, "Be angry over—and hate—the sin, but never the sinner."

Chapter 15

ARE YOU ANXIOUS OR AFRAID?

FEW OF US in these troubled times are totally immune from anxiety. Our anxieties, like our depressions, range from being merely troublesome to complete incapacitation. The answer to a life shackled by anxiety and bound by fear is faith in the Lord Jesus, for in Christ is found the answer to all things. If He were the supreme reality in our lives, if we could keep our eyes always and entirely focused on Him alone, we would keep out of trouble. Our faith would then be the power it is meant to be: not of *itself* the power to save and to heal, but the means by which we come to wholly accept Him who does both.

When we take our eyes off Christ we sink, as did Peter when he walked on the water. For just a second the disciple took His eyes off Jesus; fear immediately overcame him, and he went down (Matt. 14:30). So it is with us when the circumstances of our lives, our anxieties, frustrations, and fears, assume priority over our Lord. When they and not He become for us the great reality, we sink, drowning in their morass.

Actually, anxiety is the negation of the Spirit of God in us, for love, which *is* God, casts out fear (I John 4:18). If we loved enough or believed sufficiently in His love for us, none of us would be anxious or afraid.

I do not refer to that pathological anxiety state which is an illness. But, to the extent that the patient is able to absorb them, the same truths apply as to the "garden variety" under discussion here. For much of all anxiety derives from the past, and much is concerned with things to come. The ultimate result is that many of us have virtually no present at all.

The moment we are disobedient to God, the instant that we break a spiritual law, we suffer the consequences—which are self-induced and not God-produced. We might remember that the thrust of Christ's teaching in this regard is to live in the present, one day at a time. "Do not be anxious about tomorrow," He enjoins us. "Tomorrow will look after itself" (Matt. 6:34 N.E.B.).

Although some may live in the past and others only for the future, the Christian, in obedience to his Lord, should live in the present. He should be informed by the past, yes, but not agonized over what has been done or left undone; expectant of the future, yes, but never apprehensive over what in all probability will never come to pass. To live other than in this way—to sacrifice our present on the altar of a past filled with remorse and a future dimmed by fear—is to waste our lives.

A woman came to me in devastating remorse over the mistakes she had made in the past, beginning with her marriage some ten years before, when she had married her husband on the rebound. As a result, early in her marriage, she had taken out on her husband her unhappiness and her longing for the other man. She had two children, to whom she realized she had been a nervous and highly irritable mother.

To add to her difficulties, she had engaged in an extra-marital affair several years after her marriage. By the time she came to me she was in a pitiable state, unable to sleep, guilt-ridden and thoroughly miserable—for by now she had come to love and appreciate her husband. They could have had a happy life together, but she was so racked by regret over her past that she had neither present nor future.

She had forgotten the love and forgiveness of God. It took her approximately three months of weekly counseling to be able to accept His forgiveness and realize His absolution. At last, knowing herself cleansed and restored, she was able for the first time in ten years to live happily in the present.

Less dramatic and perhaps more frequent are cases such as that of a man who was tormenting himself because some years before he had made what proved to be an unwise business decision. He had been offered an opportunity to go with a then-new company. With a wife and three children, he had been afraid at the time to sacrifice his security for the unknown quantity of a new enterprise. The years went on. He had security but with a comparatively small salary.

The company that he had not dared join had thrived, and it was clear that had he not been afraid he would now be a wealthy man. But to all who make what appear later to be wrong decisions, whether in our business or personal lives, I would say as I did to him, "You did what seemed best to you at the time. It is done and over with. So forget it."

As for our fear of the future, most often what we fear does not come to pass. I think of a man I know who at the age of fifty-three had been let go by his company through no fault of his own. He eventually found another job, well paying but with no pension. This man had no present because he was so worried about the future.

"What will my wife and I do when I am forced to retire?" he asked in near panic. "Social Security certainly won't take care of us."

During the time that he was counseling with me, he received an unexpected inheritance from a distant relative. This, coupled with a reasonable savings plan, would enable him and his wife to live comfortably after his retirement, even if not in the style to which they had been accustomed. So his worry about the future had been in vain; in vain, that is, until he came to understand that our Lord never promised His followers cake—only bread—but the Bread of Life.

In this connection we recall again the prayer that Jesus taught us, "Give us day by day our daily bread" (Luke 11:3). There is no implication here that we should ever pray, "Give us cake and caviar and Cadillacs for the rest of our lives."

God gave us the brains we have, and He intends us to use them. In adjuring us not to worry about tomorrow, He does not mean us to do what a fanatic of my acquaintance did. This was a man with five children who interpreted our Lord's words to mean, "Don't prepare for the future." As a result, he canceled his life insurance policies. Shortly thereafter he was killed in an accident, leaving his family destitute.

This sort of irresponsibility is not what our Lord meant. He said, "Don't worry." He never said, "Don't prepare; don't carry life insurance; don't save for a rainy day."

So many of us waste half our strength in panicky anticipation of unpleasant things to come and the other half in continuing remorse over a past already gone that we have no strength left for the present. To live in this way is proof positive of our lack of trust in God.

Some chronic worriers have said to me, "You don't take into account temperamental differences. Some people are just born worriers."

Those who say this are correct: I do *not* take into account temperamental differences in this area of life. I know only too well that some people are born worriers, because I was one. If there was not something to worry about, I'd manage to manufacture something, and worry myself into a state of near collapse. But I have learned that if one is a Christian one need not remain a "born" worrier. I have learned that the best way on earth to wreck one's life is to try to take it into one's own hands, thrusting aside the hand of God, which is always there to bless, to heal, and to guide us. But we must grasp that hand when He extends it to us.

I offer here two practical suggestions. First, if you are suffering from anxiety, share your apprehension with only one person—someone you can trust. To broadcast your worries far and wide only magnifies them.

Second, practice living in what the French theologian J. P. de Caussade calls the "Sacrament of the present moment." [1] This is a difficult concept, which will take time to put into effect, but keep trying, for it is well worth the effort.

In brief, the idea consists of abandoning yourself to the will of God, moment by moment. Do not worry about His will either in retrospect or in advance; just try to live in the serenity of God's present intention for you. Center your attention on God's grace and will as they bear upon you instant by instant. Once you are centered in the present moment (neither in the past nor the future), this continuing act or surrender to Him becomes a simple, joyous, and infinitely wonderful thing. It "works," as I know from personal experience. This does not mean that in your life there will never be trouble or anxiety or tension; but it does mean that these things will be caught up in the flood of God's love and mercy, moment by moment.

[1] J. P. de Caussade, S.J., *Self Abandonment to Divine Providence* (London: Burns, Oates and Washbourne Ltd., 1959).

Anyone can learn to enter the present moment and surrender. Ask God what He wants of you now (not tomorrow or next week). Ask the Holy Spirit to open your spiritual ears so that you may hear what He is telling you.

As you gradually learn to abandon yourself to His will and plan for you, instant by instant, your remorse over the past will lessen and your worry over the future will diminish. Unimpeded by either past or future, you will find yourself living in the fullness of life in the present, and you will experience in a new way the peace of God—or, more accurately, peace *with* God.

Our Lord said, "My peace I give unto you (John 14:27). He spoke these words shortly before His betrayal and crucifixion, which He knew were shortly to occur. He spoke them to His apostles, whom He knew, as He said, "the world will hate" (John 15:19). He knew the hardship, the conflicts, the persecution which they would endure for His sake; and yet He said, "My peace I give unto you."

This is the peace which is not of this world and which has little to do with it. It is a peace that exists in your heart regardless of what has happened in the past or what may happen in the future. It is peace of mind, but far more than that. It is an ineffable peace of the heart and spirit, which comes from knowing God and striving to live according to His will. It is a peace that, regardless of trial and tribulation, lies at the core of our being, and cannot be disturbed no matter what happens to us outwardly. It is the peace that can be found only in our certain knowledge that He lives, that He dwells in us and we in Him. And so long as this is true, there is no room within us to harbor undue anxiety or fear.

As John the Baptist said, "He must increase, but I must decrease" (John 3:30). In direct proportion to His increase in our lives do we experience His peace. The key to the peace of God, as to all healing and the entire Chris-

tian life, is "Seek ye the kingdom of God" (Luke 12:31).
However, so often we believe that we *are* seeking first
the kingdom, that we *are* putting Christ first, when in
truth we are not.

In this connection I think of a devout Christian who
came to me suffering from hypertension. He appeared
nervous, and voiced extreme apprehension concerning his
job, an apprehension not for himself but for his wife. He
was fearful of being passed over for a promotion, and his
wife badly wanted the extra money this would bring. A
little sharp practice on his part, not actually cheating,
and the promotion would almost certainly be his. The
difficulty was that he was in a state of conflict, waging a
battle with his conscience.

When he asked my advice, I could only urge him to
obey his conscience, for it seemed clear to me that this
was God speaking to him. Sensing the type of person
he was, I knew that he must put God first in his life if he
were to know peace of heart. As it was, he was trying to
put his wife ahead of Christ.

I recalled to him how at the age of twelve Jesus had
lingered in the temple, badly worrying his parents, who
thought Him lost. He loved them deeply, but when His
mother chastised Him, He had to reply, "Wist ye not that
I must be about my Father's business?" (Luke 2:49).

"But I love my wife," the man said to me. Of course,
and so did Jesus love His family—but the Father had to
come first, and so it is with us.

I well knew what it would do to this man's personal
integrity were he to do what he planned to achieve the
promotion for his wife's sake. His action would destroy
not only him but also the relationship with his wife he
was so anxious to preserve. Guilt-ridden, he would never
again know God's peace, and subconsciously he would
hold his wife responsible.

I extracted a promise from the man that he would do

nothing whatsoever to further his promotion for a period of six weeks. During this time he was to pray the situation through.

Within three weeks, he called to tell me that he had been given the job he wanted without his having to make a move. As an aside, he remarked that his blood pressure was normal, which news came as no surprise.

It is just as Jesus told us: Only when we are willing to lose our life (and this includes our job and everything else we may think important) for His sake are we able to find it (Luke 9:24); and in the finding we experience that peace of God without which we cannot be truly whole.

Our Lord never promised us freedom from hardship, but He gave us Himself and His transfiguring power. He never promised that we would not have to suffer, but He gave His assurance that He would be always with us. It is through the healing ministry, where there seems such an intense awareness of His presence, that we are uniquely enabled to realize the sufficiency of this promise. It is at the altars of His healing church that we most often dare to claim it.

As we cannot receive Christ unless we first give Him ourselves, without qualification or reservation, neither can we fully experience His love for us until we give it back to Him.

"The measure you give," He says, "will be the measure you get, and still more will be given you" (Mark 4:24 R.S.V.). And the greater the intensity of our love for Him, the more of His love we are enabled to receive and then return to Him. It is a continuous cycle of giving and receiving, each time marvelously more, until at last we truly abide in Him, and *know* that He abides in us. With this inner knowing comes that peace which the world can neither give nor take away.

As our hearts come at last to rest in the knowledge that

"the eternal God is thy refuge, and underneath are the everlasting arms" (Deut. 33:27), we are able to live more nearly as He would have us to live, without anxiety or fear. We can live in the present, moment by moment, striving to know and do His will, looking neither behind with regret nor ahead with trepidation.

It is through Scripture, sacrament and prayer, through penitence and adoration, that we finally come to know Him whom we worship. Then it is that the kingdom of God becomes for us a present reality as well as a future hope. We know at last the meaning of His words, and take them to ourselves: "My peace I give unto you."

Chapter 16

GOD LOVES *YOU*

LONELINESS SEEMS TO BE one of humanity's most prevalent ailments. I consider it an "ailment" because at the least it can cause great misery for those who suffer from it, and at the most, if untended, it can lead to a deep, pathological depression.

Some time ago I took a course in which mankind's basic needs were under discussion. At the head of the list on the blackboard, the instructor had written in large white letters the word "acceptance," a popular word today, with which I take exception when used in such a context. I am convinced that it is not merely acceptance but *love* that human beings require.

In my opinion to receive love and to give love are basic needs. As Christians we can and should help those who are lonely by giving them of ourselves and our time. We can and should help those who feel themselves unloved by loving them (and letting them know it), whoever and wherever they may be.

About a year ago, a young man brought to Christ through the Calvary ministry, on fire with zeal, was transferred by his company from Pittsburgh to another city. He was a new Christian of only a few months, and during these months he had regularly attended the healing services and been deeply involved with a prayer group. Thus he had been well nurtured by his new-found Christian friends.

The day before he left Pittsburgh I talked with him and cautioned him not to be discouraged in his new environment, where he might have difficulty in finding people of like mind and spirit. As we are all aware, there is not a superabundance of committed Christians, and when we are moved to a new location, it usually takes a while to ferret them out.

I warned him against the frustration he would feel when he wanted to shout from the rooftops, "Christ lives"—and no one would listen. And I warned him against loneliness. At this he demurred. "Surely no one who knows Christ can ever be lonely," he said.

In one sense he was of course correct. The loneliness of the Christian is very different from that of the pagan. It is, in fact, a glorious thing—but nevertheless, it *is* loneliness.

Some weeks later I received a letter from this young man, telling me that he was suffering from the sense of keen frustration I had foreseen. Furthermore, he was desperately lonely, even though he knew Christ. He had not been a Christian long enough to realize the cost of the faith, and one of its costs is loneliness.

Humanly speaking, the life of the spirit is an intensely lonely one. At the core of every individual's being is an area that no other person, no matter how intimate or devoted—not even a husband or wife—can penetrate. It is an inviolable loneliness. This is true of everyone, Christian or otherwise, but it is especially true of the Christian, for Christians are *in* the world but not *of* it, and there is a constant tension involved in having one foot in heaven and the other on earth. Yet though loneliness can be a curse for the unbeliever, for the Christian it is—or can be —a blessed state, because it enables us to share in the loneliness of the Lord Jesus as He walked the earth. The "Son of Man hath not where to lay his head" (Matt. 8:20), and his disciples have always been "strangers and pilgrims on the earth" (Heb. 11:13).

But if we offer our loneliness to Christ, we are brought ever closer to the God we worship. Loneliness is part of the cross we are called upon, and deeply privileged, to carry. When we carry it in His name and for His sake, the yoke is easy and the burden light (Matt. 11:30).

Loneliness is thus a blessed state, but paradoxically it is our holy obligation to mitigate it whenever we find it in others, whether they be Christians or not, and to relieve it by the love of God manifested through us.

One evidence of loneliness is the crying need of so many to have someone to talk to, and to *listen*. I remember a winter night when my telephone rang about midnight. The call was from a distraught woman, saying she was all alone, ill, and contemplating suicide. She asked that I go to her at once.

I was in bed, it was a bad night, the roads covered with snow and ice, and the woman lived about as far from me as possible and still be in Pittsburgh. I was not overly enthusiastic at the prospect of crawling out of my warm bed and braving the elements, but sensing the urgency in her voice, I was afraid to delay my visit until morning.

When I reached my destination, I was greeted by an elderly woman, her face strained and white with evidence of recent tears. As she talked, I learned that her husband had died the year before; but it was soon evident that she had no intention of taking her life, nor was she physically ill.

My initial reaction was one of some annoyance that she had lied to me over the telephone. However, as she talked I realized that she did indeed suffer from a sickness: an intolerable loneliness, which had reached its climax at that hour, and which required alleviation as surely as any agonizing physical pain. She had stood it as long as she was able, and then her need to talk, to know that someone cared, overpowered her.

I stayed with her for nearly two hours, and it was time well spent, for I left her serene, knowing that someone was concerned. Obviously one cannot place oneself at the perpetual disposal of neurotics who make unreasonable demands. Such was not the case with this particular woman, who was, I learned later, a considerate and honest person. It was simply that on this one night her need was so overwhelming that it transcended every other consideration.

In the vast majority of cases, an occasional visit during the day to someone who needs to talk and be listened to, who needs the assurance of someone's genuine concern, can make the difference between a life of tenable contentment or one of veritable hell. To visit the lonely is such a small act of Christian service that one wishes more people would perform it and thus assist in alleviating a tiny fraction of the world's anguish.

In regard to loneliness among Christians, we see yet another paradox. The more we know of God, the more we long to know, for in direct proportion to our growing knowledge of Him is our holy desire for more and more of Him. This desire never abates as long as we live; curiously enough, as we grow in the knowledge and love of God, as we grow in the life of the spirit, so does a nostalgia, a certain kind of loneliness, increase. This is in actuality a blessing bestowed by God, for it makes us to an ever greater degree dependent upon Christ, Who is our fulfillment, and in Whom there is no aloneness at all.

Our very loneliness is part of the faith we embrace, and it paves the way to holiness. It is given real and deep meaning as it involves us increasingly more in Christ and continually throws us on His mercy and not that of other people; for it is God and God alone Whose mercy never fails us.

It is through Him that we come eventually to recognize

the difference between loneliness and aloneness, for these two words are by no means synonymous. But the remedy for both is the same: to love. And to love is also part of the cost of the faith we embrace. To love is to make oneself vulnerable to what can seem almost unbearable hurts: the love of a wife for her husband who is having an affair with another woman; the love of parents for their children who may get into serious trouble or later on neglect them; the love of friends who may let one down.

As Louis Evely asserts, "To love a person means inevitably to depend on him, it means giving him power over us. By loving us of His own free will, God has chosen to give us power over Him." [1]

Thus even God Himself is vulnerable, because He loves.

The way to help others in their loneliness is by your love. But I would go further and say that if you have never known loneliness within yourself, you cannot offer love, for you cannot feel or know—and therefore cannot meet—the deep need of the truly lonely.

"Whosoever he be of you that forsaketh not all that he hath, he cannot be my disciple," Jesus said (Luke 14:33).

This is a basic premise of the religious life as it is lived in community, but it applies equally to those of us who live in the world. This does not mean that you should neglect your family or abandon your friends or that you should love your family and friends less. It simply means that you must love God more in order to more truly love them. And as you love Him more, His grace is in your heart to minister His love to the lonely. As you come to learn your total dependence upon Him, His grace is in your eyes to minister His joy to the de-

[1] Louis Evely, *We Dare to Say Our Father* (New York: Herder and Herder, 1965), p. 45.

spairing. As you live increasingly in and for Him, His grace is on your lips to minister His peace. For again, paradoxically, while the life of the spirit is in a sense a lonely one, you possess that glorious knowledge, of heart and mind and spirit, that in and with Him there can be no real *aloneness* at all.

"And the Lord God said, It is not good that man should be alone" (Gen. 2:18). Unless we are called to live the life of a desert hermit, which is not likely in this day and age, we should be able to depend at least to some extent upon our fellow human beings to alleviate the human loneliness that is the lot of many who are alone in the world. If you are a Christian, you will know yourself bound to your fellow Christians in the strongest of bonds—that of the Holy Spirit, by Whom all Christians are made one in Christ. But however true this is, and however effectively your association with other Christians may mitigate your loneliness, what about the aloneness from which you may suffer and which no one can relieve, if you do not know in your heart the reality of the love of God?

We hear the words "the love of God" so often without really knowing what they mean that this phrase has become for many of us merely a pious cliché. It was so with me long after I had become a Christian, until that never-to-be-forgotten day when I first experienced the supranatural love of God as I laid hands on a man suffering from a critical heart ailment. In the middle of the healing prayer there was such an awareness of the presence of Christ and His overwhelming love that I could not continue the vocal prayer. His love flooded the room. After kneeling by the sick man's bed and offering thanksgiving, he turned to me with a look of extraordinary radiance, and said, "Today I have known God." And so had I.

Many people claim that we can know the love of God

only as it is manifested through other human beings. This is only half true: We can experience His love directly in circumstances such as I have just described, and which since then have been repeated countless times both for me and for many.

So often people say to me, "How can *I* experience the love of God of which you speak?" First, every healing service in which I participate seeks, through God, to give this experience to those who attend: To know the love of Christ in this way is in reality to experience God Himself, who *is* love. And this, as far as I am concerned, is the primary purpose of the healing ministry. Second, the full answer to this question can be given only by the Holy Spirit Himself. It is because His presence is so peculiarly intensified at healing services that I urge people to attend on a regular basis. The average person gradually grows in receptivity, until at last he is able to receive that which God is so eager to give, namely, Himself—and with Himself comes that abundant life promised by our Lord (John 10:10).

Sometimes the reality of the love of God comes to us during prayer as a sudden revelation, but most often it is a gradual process, a slow and sometimes painful opening of our hearts and understanding by the Holy Spirit, who, if we will only permit Him, stands ready to lead us unerringly into all truth—the love of God and the kingdom disclosed by Jesus. We are far from understanding *how*, but we know a little of *what* is necessary on our part if we are to experience God. One thing of which we are sure is that if we love God only when things go well, only for the material happiness He has given us, only for the healing He proffers us in the name of Jesus, we are not really loving God at all; we are loving only His gifts. We truly love God only when we can say with Saint Ignatius, "Give me only Thy love and Thy grace. With Thee I am rich enough nor do I ask for aught besides."

We must believe with our hearts that "God so loved the world, that He gave His only begotten Son" (John 3:16). These words are so familiar that they tend to fall on deaf ears. What, actually, do they mean to you?

They mean that the Son of God gave Himself not for an impersonal world, a faceless mass of humanity, but for *you*. It is as Saint Paul says: "The Son of God who loved me, and gave himself for me" (Gal. 2:20).

He knows each of His sheep by name, and this means *you*. He knows and cares about *you* so much that He knows the number of hairs on your head (Matt. 10:30). When He says, "Come unto me" (Matt. 11:28), He is calling *you*.

Once your heart can truly perceive the fact that God loves *you* in the most profound and personal way, your battle against aloneness is half won. Total victory lies in your response to His love, thus fulfilling your need to love as well as to be loved.

"We love him, because he first loved us" (I John 4:19). Now at last you have empirical knowledge of this statement. You finally know in your innermost being that God loves *you* and not just "us." You are then able to respond emotionally to His love, thus setting in motion the whole process of the love of God, the mystical exchange of His love for us and ours for Him.

"We have known and believed the love that God hath to us. God is love; and he that dwelleth in love dwelleth in God and God in him" (I John 4:16). In this mutual abiding lies an everlasting divine companionship and the end forever of our aloneness.

Chapter 17

THE BODY OF CHRIST

THE STATE OF MOST CHURCHES today ranges from confusion to chaos. The decline in church attendance is attributed to the fact that the church is not relevant to this age—a charge that is being met alternately or simultaneously by an often extreme liberalism, exaggerated social activism, and changes of liturgy that seek to update and modernize our worship. Notwithstanding all these efforts, millions are turning to the occult. Surely this is saying something that the church is failing to hear.

The charge that the established church is obsolete and not geared to meet the needs of this sophisticated and scientifically oriented era seems curious as we observe the practices that great masses of people now consider "relevant" to their needs: astrology, spiritualism, and witchcraft, all of which predate Christianity by thousands of years. The name of Sybil Leek, present-day "good" witch and high priestess of the occult, is as well known to millions, and better known to many, as that of Saint Paul; countless individuals now turn to the Ouija board for guidance rather than to the Holy Spirit; and the cult of satanism grows by leaps and bounds. In view of such religious regression I can only believe the church errs in attempting to solve her problems by striving to "update" the faith. Her structure may change, but never the gospel.

Many who have left their churches have remarked to me, "The church is dead, and besides, who needs it? All that matters to me is my own personal relationship with Jesus." This is not the Christian faith, for one cannot be a Christian alone. All Christians are together in Christ, members incorporate of His mystical body, which is "the blessed company of all faithful people" (B.C.P., p. 83). We can imagine Saint Paul's reaction had one of his converts come to him and said, "Paul, I believe in the crucified and risen Christ whom you preach—but I don't care to be a member of His body, the church."

The salvation of our own souls is certainly a matter of inexpressible importance, but as Christians we cannot stop there. We cannot be satisfied that we, individually, have accepted our salvation, and live out our lives basking exclusively in the glory of our intimate personal relationship with our Lord. The primacy of the individual at the expense of the body was never the teaching of the ancient, power-filled church. As Saint Paul says, "None of us lives to himself, and none of us dies to himself" (Rom. 14:7). We can only partake of the blessed freedom of God in the measure that we are concerned with the salvation of others. Those who are free in Christ *must* be concerned with others.

"I have become all things to all men, that I might by all means save some," says the apostle (I Cor. 9:22). In his concern for the salvation of others, he even goes so far as to say he would forfeit his own salvation if by so doing he could bring others to Christ (Rom. 9:3).

Frequently I come upon those who are interested only in their own relationship with God, and I know from what I have observed that if we reject the corporate and institutional side of the church, nothing can keep any of us from a narrow intensity; from an overemphasis on certain aspects of the faith; from a basic uncharitableness. The ultimate result of such rejection seems to be inevitably, as Von Hugel says, "a shifting subjectivity, and all but incurable tyranny of mood and fancy: fanaticism is in full sight." [1]

"I will give thanks unto the Lord with my whole heart, secretly among the faithful, and in the congregation" (Ps. 111:1). All over the world, small groups of the faithful are meeting for prayer and study. These groups are a happy compromise between the impersonality of today's large churches and the "lone wolf" Christian. Here deep spiritual needs are met and great spiritual power released. However, these groups should never serve as a substitute for the church, but as a supplement to it.

The ever-increasing number of persons who are turning to the Far Eastern religions are in revolt against today's materialism. They hunger for the mysticism which is actually a part of the Christian heritage; yet the church does not proffer the spiritual treasure she possesses. When she refuses to offer that which is uniquely hers to give, she falls far behind the times because of her very effort to keep up with them. In her tendency to believe that the faith once delivered (Jude: 3) is meaningless and irrelevant today, the church, in my opinion, fails to meet the spiritual needs of her people because she has misinterpreted them. She has sought to feed her people by becoming increasingly secularized, when it is in the field of the spirit that they are starving. It is not good works alone, however important, or new liturgies, however welcome, that will bring the young and not so young back to our churches; it is the evidence that Christ still lives.

[1] Baron Von Hugel, *Spiritual Counsel and Letters,* Douglas V. Steere, ed. (New York: Harper and Row, 1964), p. 132.

At one of the services in a recent healing mission in New York was a girl in her early twenties, obviously a hippie. I was to learn that she attended a Buddhist temple. What then was she doing at a Christian healing mission?

She suffered from a cruel form of arthritis that afflicts the young, and was unable to move without the help of a walker. She had been raised as a Christian but had long since abandoned the faith. Her family's pastor had prevailed upon her to attend the healing service, to which she had agreed out of sheer desperation.

She was marvelously healed that night. The following morning she got out of bed and walked unaided. But the healing of the spirit she received at the altar rail was far more significant than her physical healing, wonderful as it was.

She told me that as she received the laying on of hands, she saw a great blinding light, and she was conscious of a Presence so real she felt it almost palpable. Suddenly she knew Who that presence was, and she called Him by name: Jesus, her Saviour and Redeemer.

The pastor of the mission church knew little of the healing ministry, and he later confessed that he and his wife had discussed the healing of this girl at great length. Why was *she* healed, they wondered, while other long-committed Christians had perhaps remained unhealed?

The answer seemed to me very clear: This girl had been healed that she might go home and tell her friends what great things the Lord had done for her (Mark 5:19). This is precisely what she did, and many of her friends were brought to Christ through her witness.

Then there was the night at Calvary when I found a young man waiting to speak to me after the service. He was a postgraduate student at the University of Pittsburgh, where he led a free-thinking movement. On his way home he had seen the lights in the church, and out of curiosity (and also because he was cold) he had stopped by.

He claimed that the moment he entered the church, he "felt" something he had never experienced before. Just when he had decided it must be his imagination, the laying on of hands began. Something seemed to push him to his knees, and as he knelt alone in a rear pew, he experienced God. He knew beyond the shadow of any doubt the reality of Christ.

It was difficult for the young man to tell me this, and even more difficult for him to say, "I know now I've been on the wrong track. I want to learn all I can about the Christian faith."

For many weeks this young man returned, each time bringing a friend. He is now a Christian leader on campus.

For these young people and the many others like them, the Christian faith is highly relevant; it has changed their lives.

I think of the young woman who had never heard of the healing ministry until two weeks after her husband died. Someone told her of the services at Calvary, and she came, distraught, grief-stricken, frightened, desolate beyond description.

Week after week she came, as we claimed His promise to bind up the broken-hearted (Isa. 61:1), to give that peace which only He can give. We prayed that she might receive the full grace and consolation of His Holy Spirit; that He guide her along the paths He wanted her to walk in, and open those doors through which He wanted her to pass. We watched with awe as God worked in the life of this woman, and we saw her made whole again in Him. What could be more relevant than this?

Then there was the hard-headed businessman who

came to a healing service at Calvary at the instigation of his wife. He had scheduled a vitally important business meeting in New York two days later, and he came to the altar rail asking the guidance and blessing of God.

The meeting was successful beyond his company's greatest expectation. When he was complimented on how he had handled the conference, his response was "I didn't; God did." Ask *this* man whether or not the faith is relevant.

And what could be more "relevant" to the countless sick who have been restored to health through the healing ministry? Through this ministry innumerable people have learned for the first time something of the power and glory of God. Many for the first time have experienced something of the infinity of His love that is Himself, who alone can make us and the world whole. And what can be more relevant than this?

I believe that many and probably most of the world's problems are spiritually based. Prejudice is one example. Prejudice cannot be *legislated* out of people, nor can it be *reasoned* out. It is a spiritual problem. All of us have some prejudice in some area of our lives, and all of us need the reconciling touch of Christ upon our spirits if we are to be healed.

To the extent that we are prejudiced, or greedy, or bigoted, or hateful, to that extent are we separated from God and "there is no health in us" (B.C.P., p. 23). Again, it is the living, healing Christ alone Who can deliver us. And in His deliverance we are aware once more of the eternal relevance of the faith.

Often after a healing service at Calvary someone new to the services will say, "I plan to come here every Monday night instead of going to my own church on Sunday. I've been here three times and I get so much more out of *these* services."

However happy I am to be told that the healing services are meaningful, such a comment always disturbs me. Everyone is welcome at Calvary, believers and skeptics, the churched and the unchurched. We pray always that the skeptics will become believers, and the unchurched, churched. But those who come to Calvary who are members of a church should never substitute healing services for Sunday worship. However dynamic and important it may be, the healing ministry is only one of the ministries of the church.

To fail to attend church on Sundays is to remove oneself from the worshiping Body. We go to church on Sundays for one purpose alone: to worship almighty God as His people. Our motivation should not be "what we get," but the giving of ourselves. And in the giving, we receive Him whom we worship.

This of course obtains whether or not we are sacramentalists. However, as a sacramentalist myself I am acutely aware of the fact that it is in the congregation of the people of God that the church administers the sacraments. Our Lord said, "Feed my sheep" (John 21:16). Although our spiritual nourishment consists of both word and sacrament, to attend a church where the sacrament of holy communion is offered and claim at the same time to be spiritually unfed seems to me an irreconcilable contradiction.

However imperfect the institutional church may be, she still offers more to her people than any other agency on earth. In my opinion, the church errs if she believes the only way to be meaningful in this era is to concentrate exclusively on social action. Yet this is not to say that she should not concern herself with the world and its problems. Obviously she must, as did Christ Himself, who mingled with drunkards and was Himself accused of being a wine-bibber, who associated with prostitutes and all sorts of undesirable people. He is no less today in and with alcoholics and junkies and hippies.

The church must be found, as is her Lord, wherever there is pain, and this she is making heroic efforts to do. Whatever her faults, complacency is not among them, for she is her own severest critic.

Many spiritually gifted individuals are impatient with what they feel to be the slowness of the church, her failure to keep pace with *them*. Yet on the whole, I have found the church to be a wise mother who recognizes the danger of being "tossed to and fro, and carried about with every wind and doctrine" (Eph. 4:14).

It has become increasingly clear, however, that the church can never again retreat to her ivory tower of aloof "otherness," apparently forgetting that Christ died for all men and that He looks with compassion upon the suffering world. But neither should she over-correct her former position by plunging headlong into almost total secularism, forgetting that she is Christ on earth today doing all that she does in His name; for He is her center, her heart, and her head, still reconciling man to God.

More and more churches are achieving balance by becoming involved in the healing ministry. They recognize in this ministry not only a means of reconciliation, but a powerful instrument of spiritual renewal, by which the Holy Spirit is revitalizing, revivifying, and restoring to the Church her long-diminished spiritual power.

There are those who say the church has failed. While it is true that some of the clergy and laity alike (both of whom comprise the church) have failed—the one to preach the living Christ and the other to hear—the church herself cannot fail. She is the Mystical Body of which we are all members, and Christ the Head (Col. 1:18); she is the Bride of Christ, and as such, one with Him (Rev. 21:2); she is the risen Christ among us, and Christ can neither fail nor die.

The church has been called a hospital for sinners. We

all need this hospital, for we cannot survive without its care.

The church is the dispenser of the sacraments, without which many of us could not live, nor would we want to.

Christ loved and for which He gave Himself (Eph. 5:25),

The church is the household of God (Eph. 2:17–22). We cannot exist as Christians outside the fold of this household.

If we are not members of the body, the church that we cannot call ourselves Christians. And we are not good Christians unless we contribute our prayers and our spirituality, such as it is, to the body, unless we uphold the church of Christ as He, through His church, continually upholds us.

Chapter 18

THE CHARISMATIC REVIVAL

SPIRITUALLY SPEAKING, we are living today in wonderful, exciting, and curiously paradoxical times. On the one hand, many are predicting the demise of the institutional church, while on the other, we are witnessing extraordinary manifestations of the Holy Spirit which bring joy to the heart of every believer. Yet our joy is tempered by the knowledge that from time to time throughout the history of the church there have been comparable periods of holy fire that have flamed through Christendom, only to burn out because of our abuse of the gifts bestowed upon us by the Holy Spirit of God.

These same abuses and excesses are once again becoming all too evident. However, if we are fully aware of the dangers confronting us, there is no reason why the dismal history of the past need be repeated. It is to call attention to these dangers that I write this chapter, in the hope and with the prayer that if we pay heed, we may see in our time the genuine beginning of Joel's prophecy: "And it shall come to pass, that I will pour out my Spirit upon all flesh" (Joel 2:28).

What is known as the charismatic movement has become, in many minds, erroneously synonymous with glossolalia (speaking in unknown tongues). Actually, the charismata applies to *all* the gifts of the spirit as enumerated by Saint Paul in the twelfth chapter of his First Epistle to the Corinthians, of which many are being manifested today.

The apostle makes clear that the Holy Spirit "distributes different gifts to different people, just as he chooses" (I Cor. 12:11 Jer.). In other words, all Christians do not necessarily have all or the same gifts of the Spirit (Rom. 12:6). However, all do have, by virtue of their baptism, the gift of the Spirit Himself.

"Ye shall receive power after that the Holy Ghost has come upon you," our Lord said (Acts 1:8). It is the Holy Spirit *Himself*—the third person of the Trinity—who enables, empowers, and fills us with all joy, not His gifts. The gifts edify and strengthen the church, but they are not essential to her existence; only the Holy Spirit is indispensable.

For years we have neglected the work of the Holy Spirit. We have used His name as a sort of eccesiastical "roger" or sign-off to our prayers. We didn't really know, or think about, just who the Holy Spirit is. The result is that today, with our new knowledge, many of us tend to overreact. For example, a man remarked to me not long ago, "Of course the Holy Spirit is *central.*" My reply was a quick "No." He is *not* central; He is co-equal and co-eternal with the Father and the Son, God active in our lives.

The Holy Spirit is the power of the Trinity. He was active in our Lord's earthly life from beginning to end. By His power Jesus was conceived (Luke 1:35); by His power the healing miracles were performed (Acts 10:38); by His power Christ was raised from the dead

(Rom. 8:11). Nevertheless, it is not the Holy Spirit but Jesus Christ who is central to our faith.

"When the Spirit of truth comes he will lead you to complete truth," our Lord says. "He will glorify me since all he tells you will be taken from what is mine" (John 16:13, 14 Jer.).

The neo-Pentecostal movement is now sweeping the established church; and yet this, too, is a misnomer. The true Pentecostal experience is not speaking in an unknown or nonexistent tongue; it is speaking in a foreign language intellectually unknown to the speaker. The Holy Spirit speaks through him to others in their own language so that the Word of God may be understood by the listener.

It was thus on the day of Pentecost nearly two thousand years ago, when those gathered together with one accord in one place "were all filled with the Holy Ghost, and began to speak with other tongues, as the Spirit gave them utterance—and the multitude were confounded, because that every man heard them speak in his own language" (Acts 2:4, 6).

So it was with Saint Francis Xavier, the great sixteenth-century missionary priest. Wherever he traveled in foreign lands, he preached the gospel, and although he had no conscious knowledge of the language of those to whom he preached, he was understood by all. And so it happens occasionally today. A missionary in the Far East, for example, with scant knowledge of the language of the people, immediately upon his arrival begins to preach the gospel fluently and flawlessly in their own tongue. *This* is the real Pentecostal experience.

On that day of the first Pentecost, Peter said, "Repent, and be baptized every one of you in the Name of Jesus Christ for the remission of your sins, and ye shall receive the gift of the Holy Ghost." Then Peter goes on to say, "For the promise is unto you, and to your children" (Acts 2:38, 39); and this means *us*—you and me.

According to Scripture, then, when you are baptized you receive the Holy Spirit, and thus it is erroneous to regard glossolalia as the sole sign of having received the Spirit of God. Years ago when I talked with the Reverend Dennis Bennett, one of the outstanding leaders in the tongues revival, he was in accord with me that the movement needed a new vocabulary. In his recent excellent book on glossolalia he asks the reader to "please bear with us, and don't be thrown off the track by terminology." [1] Nevertheless, many Christians *are* antagonized on a semantic basis, and one would hope for the evolvement of a more accurate terminology that would allay much criticism of the movement. Even a cursory study of Scripture is sufficient to make apparent this need.

For instance, the phrase "baptism in (of) the Spirit" when referring to speaking in tongues is never used in the New Testament. The apostolic teaching on this point is clear: There are not two baptisms, one of water and one of the Spirit. There is only one baptism. "By one Spirit," St. Paul says, "are we all baptized into one body" (I Cor. 12:13). "There is one Lord, one faith, one baptism" (Eph. 4:5).

To fail to appropriate the Spirit after our baptism, to fail to acknowledge Him, to refuse His leading, are to "quench the Spirit," against which Scripture warns us (I Thess. 5:19). Receiving the Holy Spirit is not a once-and-for-all experience. Every Christian throughout his life should pray for more and more of Him—and as our Lord promises, He shall be given to them that ask (Luke 11:13). Beyond a doubt there is a specific religious experience that for lack of a better name we call the baptism of the Spirit. This consists of a peculiarly vivid infilling of the Spirit, with or without the manifestation

[1] Dennis Bennett, *Nine O'clock in the Morning* (Logus International, 1970), p. 2, footnote.

of tongues. There are continual infillings of the Spirit which may be less dramatic but are nonetheless powerful, so that whatever our task, we are enabled and strengthened by Him to perform it in Jesus' name. The doctrine of the Holy Spirit gradually unfolds in the Old Testament and reaches full development in the New Testament, where since the time of Christ the gift of the Holy Spirit is the gift of the Third Person of the Trinity within the life of every believer—the gift of the risen Lord, given two thousand years ago, and given still to as many as will receive Him, that He may reside in all of us who belong to Christ, controlling and ruling our lives. All who try to follow our Lord, walking in the Spirit as Saint Paul enjoins us (Gal. 5:16), have the valid seal of the Spirit upon their lives.

The phenomenon of glossolalia as it is occurring today has scriptural authority (I Cor. 12:10), and accompanying it is that tremendous joy that comes when there is manifested within us any one of His gifts. No one knows this better than I; however, I can only deplore the fact that the overzealous so frequently equate possession of the Holy Spirit with tongues.

Many have come to me in deep distress because they do not speak in tongues and have been told that they therefore lack the Spirit. This is wholly untrue, and when they say, as did one man who came all the way from California to discuss the matter, "But how can I *know* if I have the Spirit of God?" the answer is "If you manifest in your life the fruit of the Spirit" (Gal. 5:22, 23).

The term Spirit-filled Christian in Pentecostal language means *only* the believer who speaks in tongues, and this is still another error. The evidence of the Spirit-filled believer lies in the fruit and the power of the Spirit, not in the manifestation of tongues. To claim otherwise is unscriptural, for as Anglican priest Michael Harper (who himself speaks in tongues) states, "The only Scriptural evidence [of the correlation of tongues and the Spirit] we have at our disposal is a series of incidents in the Book of Acts, and even this slender documentation is not conclusive."[2] Larry Christenson, Lutheran pastor and a leader in the glossolalia movement, also concedes that a dogmatic case cannot be made on the basis of New Testament evidence.[3]

As I see so many around me running from meeting to meeting frenetically striving to acquire tongues, I am torn between joy that so many want more of God and apprehension as to *why* they are seeking this particular gift rather than, let us say, the gift of wisdom. I think it behooves us all to carefully check our motives. Have we a sincere desire to strengthen the Body of Christ, regardless of the cost to ourselves? Or could it be that we are seeking so frantically simply for our own self-gratification? Could it be, as I heard one man honestly state, our desire or what we think is our need to "blow off steam"? Could it be the weakness of our faith, which demands a "sign"? Could it be that we seek an emotional "kick" or wish to seem more "spiritual," more favored by God, than others? The answers to these questions will be given us in quiet prayer.

The gifts of the Spirit are for Christian service and vary in the faithful according to God's purpose for each individual; however, *gifts* and *service* are not in themselves evidence of spirituality. The church in Corinth had the gift of tongues, yet this church was carnal and corrupt, grossly misusing the gift. This is precisely why Saint Paul devoted so much space to the subject in his First Epistle to the Corinthians.

Today the situation in many of our churches is much the same as at Corinth. Tongues too often have proved

   [2] Michael Harper, *Walk in the Spirit* (London: Hodder and Stoughton, 1968), p. 20.
   [3] Larry Christenson, *Speaking in Tongues, A Gift for the Body of Christ* (Foundation Trust, 1963), p. 14.

destructively divisive, splitting churches between the "haves" and the "have nots"; and many who speak in tongues are manipulative and spiritually arrogant. In such cases one must conclude that the phenomenon of glossolalia is not always of God. We should never overlook those involved in the charismatic revival who are keenly aware of the abuses within the movement, who are amenable to suggestion and criticism, who are perpetually vigilant against spiritual pride and honestly striving to work within the framework of the church. To such as these, we all owe a debt of gratitude.

As there are dangers in the healing ministry, so there are dangers in tongues: the danger of overemphasis, of seeking the gift rather than the Giver, of inducing tongues, thus removing it from the category of a gift of God to a mere psychological phenomenon. There is also grave jeopardy for the emotionally unstable, who avidly seeking the gift, cannot handle it and are often thrown alarmingly from what may be a mild neurosis into a real psychosis. In Christian concern we should be aware of the gravity of this risk; we should always be cautious and not insistently attempt to thrust what for us has proved a blessing upon another for whom it may be a curse and contrary to God's will.

It is natural enough for us who have received any of the gifts to be enthusiastic over our blessing, to want not only to share our experience but also, in our zeal, to see everyone with whom we come in contact receive the same blessing. This, however, is not within our province, but God's. If we refuse to open our eyes to this fact we are guilty of the sin of presumption and pride, and ours is the guilt of working against the will of God. Far from manifesting the fruit of the Spirit, we may cause irreparable damage to others. This danger obtains with *all* the gifts of the Spirit, all of which are subject to abuse.

There are those, for example, who claim the gift of

healing and refuse to work under the authority of the church. I know too many such individuals who make the rounds of hospitals, unasked, and laying hands on a hapless patient, say, "Now you're healed. Go home."

If the invalid is very ill and sufficiently gullible to believe he is healed and leaves the hospital, the chances are excellent that he will die. If he refuses and happens to die in the hospital, his family is often assailed by feelings of intolerable guilt. "If only we had stepped out on faith," they say in agonized remorse. "If only we had claimed his healing and taken him home, he would be alive today."

Then there is exorcism, which is part of the healing picture. In my opinion, this is dangerous and should never be done lightly. If time and circumstances allow, it should be done under controlled conditions. Nor should it be done indiscriminately, but only if an individual requests it. Yet there are those who habitually tell anyone who is ill or disturbed that he or she is demon-possessed. They then proceed immediately, with no preparation, to exorcise the patient. When he fails to respond, he now has to struggle not only with illness but also with the idea that he is possessed. Thus his last state is infinitely worse than his first.

In many charismatic groups there seems to be an undue emphasis on Satan, an emphasis that culminates in the age-old heresy of dualism, where Satan and God are considered co-equal adversaries.

Personally, I find it impossible not to believe in Satan. But to consider him equally powerful with God, who in Christ has won the victory, is inconsistent with the Christian faith. Satan is strong, yes, but he exists by God's permission, and his power is strictly limited. As he was overcome by Jesus, so he continues to be overcome as we call upon the protection of our Lord.

To refuse to acknowledge that Satan exists seems to

me to fall into his trap. To make him the scapegoat for our personal sins is an easy way out of individual responsibility. To concentrate on him equally with and sometimes to the virtual exclusion of God is heresy.

I remember well my discomfiture when I found myself inadvertently participating in a small healing service with someone who seemed greatly overfocused on Satan. We both laid hands on each supplicant, alternating our prayers. Not once did my partner mention the name of God affirmatively: Each prayer dealt exclusively with casting out Satan.

The gift of prophecy likewise is subject to dangerous abuse. I know many with a genuine gift in the New Testament sense of delivering God's message to us today. Yet I know others who claim the gift of prophecy who are doing untold harm. These will say, for example, to one who is very ill, "The Lord told me that on April thirteenth at five in the afternoon, you will be healed."

These self-termed prophets leave in their wake an anguished trail of unfulfillment. The gullible, made so by desperation, are crushed by bewildered disappointment when the predicted healing fails to occur on schedule. Not only should *no one* have the temerity to set dates and times of healing, but no one should ever *promise* a physical healing to anyone.

Someone has said, "The corruption of the best, is the worst," and so it is with the gifts of the Spirit. Those who are peculiarly open to the Holy Spirit are also open to evil spirits—and every gift can be emulated by Satan.

I have mentioned the excesses in those areas that come most often to my attention, and I have seen the damage caused to many lives. I have seen the emotional disturbances, the mental derangements, the harm done the physically sick by the abuse of the gifts. I have seen spiritual pride engendered in the cults that have begun outside the church, because "the Holy Spirit is not operative in our church and certainly not in our pastor. Therefore we meet at our homes instead, where He *is* operative." I have seen countless marriages destroyed because the partner of the one who has a particular gift has not the same gift. All these things are particularly heinous because they are done ostensibly in the name of Jesus.

During the past few years thousands have been blessed by one or more gifts of the Spirit through which the church has been edified. However, if the present trend toward prostitution of the gifts continues, if we fail to exercise due vigilance, I am fearful that what might have been an unprecedented and glorious outpouring of His Spirit upon all flesh may end instead in ever more ungodly and ungovernable excesses. Then it will be as Carl Jung has said of the past: "Fanaticism is always a sign of suppressed doubt. Always in those times when the Church begins to waver, the style becomes fanatical or fanatical sects spring up, because the secret doubt has to be quenched. When one is really convinced, one is perfectly calm and can discuss one's belief as a personal point of view without any particular resentment." [4]

If we follow as the Spirit of God leads us into all truth, we will never take our eyes from the Lord Jesus. If we strive to follow Him, to align our wills with His, we can come to no harm, nor will we ever harm others in misguided zeal. We will come to know with Saint Paul that the greatest of all His gifts is love, the "more excellent" way of which the apostle speaks (I Cor. 13:1). Prophecies shall fail, he tells us; tongues shall cease and knowledge will vanish away (I Cor. 13:8). Only faith, hope, love, will abide, and the greatest of these is love (I Cor. 13:13).

[4] C. J. Jung, *Analytical Psychology: Its Theory and Practice* (New York: Pantheon Books, 1968), p. 172.

Chapter 19

SUGGESTIONS FOR THE LAY PERSON WHO WOULD MINISTER TO OTHERS

THE HEALING MINISTRY is a costly ministry for all who participate in it in any way: for those who seek healing for themselves; for those who intercede for others; for those who minister in any kind of public capacity. It is costly in terms of involvement and selflessness, for it is a fellowship of the truly concerned. At the same time, it can be the most rewarding of all ministries for the lay person.

While love is not confined to the Christian, it is as Dietrich Bonhoeffer says: "Human love is directed to the other person for his own sake; spiritual love loves him for Christ's sake." [1] And so it is with those in this min-

[1] Quoted in *The Little Chronicle*, Oct., 1970, a Society of St. Francis publication.

159

istry. They who know the healing Christ have a strong desire to take their knowledge and love out into the world, to minister for His sake to suffering friends and neighbors. Almost daily, lay people query me as to how this may best be done. I address myself here to some questions frequently asked.

(1) "How should I approach the sick who may know nothing of, or do not believe in, the healing ministry?"

The thing *not* to do is to assault the patient with your knowledge that Christ heals. If you do this, you are likely to frighten the patient, who will think you know something about his condition which he has not been told; or you will so thoroughly antagonize him that you will never be able to convey your message.

When asked to visit such an individual by believing (or desperate) members of his family, I have found the best procedure is to go quietly into the sickroom, visiting casually and briefly. When it is almost time to leave, broach the subject by asking, "Do you know anything about the healing ministry?"

If the answer is "No," remind the patient that more than one-third of the gospels is devoted to our Lord's earthly healing ministry, and that it is recorded that He healed all who came to Him. Remind the patient that He is the same yesterday, today, and forever (Heb. 13:8); ell him briefly of the early post-apostolic church, in which healing was expected and received; explain today's revival of the church's ministry of healing and mention some of the wonderful things that are happening as a result. If you feel an impulse to pray for the sick person, ask if you may do so. In the majority of cases the patient is delighted. If members of the family are present, suggest that they (and the patient if he is able) might like to do some further reading concerning the healing ministry, and leave with them some pamphlets and a list of books. Suggest to the family that they attend healing services as intercessors.

If you find the patient alone when you visit, offer not only to hold him in prayer during the week but to attend healing services on his behalf, and ask him to be in prayer at approximately the same time. To offer yourself as intercessor, praying that you will be an open channel for God's healing power, is at once a high calling and the sacred duty of all Christians.

If, however, when you ask the patient if he knows anything about the healing ministry he replies, "Yes— and I don't believe a word of it," this is your cue to strike a light note. In such cases I have found it helpful to say something like, "Well, *I* believe in it. I *have* to on the basis of Scripture and what I've seen happen in so many lives." Then I go on, "How about indulging *me*, even if *you* don't believe, and letting me say a prayer with you?"

I have had some amusing experiences with this approach. In one case, for example, a man whose wife had asked me to visit him watched television the entire time I was praying. Nonetheless, this man, who was critically ill, took a dramatic turn for the better two hours later. Healings under these conditions lead to the next question.

(2) "How important is the faith of the person who is ill?"

This question I have discussed earlier in some detail. Suffice it to say here that, while helpful, it is not necessarily essential. However, there must be faith *somewhere*. The man who watched television during the healing prayer may have had little or no faith, but *I*, who was ministering to him, believed. With the very sick we should not demand a miracle-working faith, for this takes an energy they do not possess. Rather should we who believe offer to exercise faith for them.

(3) "Should I lay hands on the sick?"

This is a question which, in my opinion, cannot be answered by a categorical "Yes" or "No." The laying on of hands, while itself not a sacrament, is a sacramental rite, and therefore should not be used indiscriminately by people who have no concept of what they are doing or why; nor should it be received by individuals without some explanation, lest the healing rite be misconstrued as magic. Incalculable harm has been done the healing ministry by those who have great zeal but no knowledge.

It is my belief that those who feel a vocation to lay on hands should do so always under the aegis of the church. In the healing ministry, one is handling the power of God, and this requires emotional balance—a balance that seems to me virtually impossible to maintain without the stabilizing influence of the church. In general, the safest rule to follow is simply to pray, holding the hand of the patient. If the one in need is a member of your own family, by all means lay on hands whether or not you feel you have a "vocation"; for love is the greatest healing force on earth.

(4) "What about ministering to someone who is unconscious?"

Talk and act with him as if he could hear every word you say. Take his hand if you can; explain briefly about the healing Christ, the will of God for wholeness, His power to mend all brokenness. Then offer aloud your prayer for healing.

There have been occasions when I have done this and a nurse has walked into the room. Clearly thinking me mentally incompetent, she has said, "Don't you know this patient is in a coma and can't hear a word you say?" I just nod and go on praying, for there have been numerous times when a patient emerges from his coma days later and remembers every word and prayer that has been uttered. The ears may not hear at the time, but the spirit never sleeps and is never unconscious.

I recall vividly the case of a man desperately ill whom I had visited several times. The man knew his condition, and in talking with me remarked that he had never had an experience of God and was afraid to die. With these words, he lapsed into a coma.

I drew up a chair close to his bed and read to him portions of Scripture. Then I asked the unconscious man to picture our Lord at sundown at the end of a long day. Jesus was very tired, and when He came out from the house in which He was staying, He saw the streets lined with pallets on which lay the sick and dying. Our Lord forgot His fatigue, and in mercy and love He ministered to each and every one, and all were made whole (Luke 4:4).

I spoke a few words about the love God held for the sick man lying in a coma, of how He knew exactly what was happening, and even then stood beside the bed, stretching out His hand to heal. Then I left the room.

The next morning the man's wife called me, her voice jubilant. Her husband had recovered consciousness and had asked to see me. That afternoon I found him sitting up in bed, his face radiant. His first words were, "I experienced the love of God last night. Never have I known such joy and peace." Then he went on to say, "How could anyone knowing this love ever be afraid to die? I know I'm not anymore."

This man did not die; from that day on he made a swift and uneventful recovery. This episode leads into questions concerning death and the healing ministry which are frequently asked, and which we should be prepared to answer.

Not long ago I received a letter from a mother whose little girl had recently died. The person who had ministered to the child before her death had commented that we are with Jesus, whether on earth or in heaven. The mother asked, quite logically, "Why then do we pray for healing on this earth?"

My answer to her, as to all who ask this question, was

to this effect: God has given us life for a purpose, and it is our obligation to seek to preserve that life. We are called to emulate as closely as possible the healing work of our Lord. Therefore we pray for the healing of the sick, following as best we can the example of His ministry of healing set before us in the gospel.

Some time ago I heard a gentleman make a remark I have never forgotten. "If I live," he said, "Christ is with me; if I die, I am with Him." These are the words of someone who knows and loves his Lord. It is the expression of that knowledge universally held by the early Christians which accounts for their joy in the face of death. It is another way of stating Saint Paul's sentiments when the apostle says, "For me to live is Christ, and to die is gain. For I am in a strait betwixt the two, having a desire to depart, and to be with Christ; which is far better. Nevertheless to abide in the flesh is more needful for you" (Phil. 1:21–24).

We pray for healing not because we fear death, but in obedience to our Lord's command to heal the sick; and with the realization that the life we pray for, whether ours or someone else's, may be "more needful" here on earth.

A common question was voiced by a woman recently widowed who said, "I have been told that prayer lengthened my husband's life by at least two years, but during these two years, he suffered greatly. Wouldn't it have been better if we had not prayed, and he had died before he began to suffer?"

To me a question of this kind carries with it the inference that prayer is some sort of magic, or else is offered to change the mind of God. Prayer is not magic, and the mind of God cannot be changed. Had God not willed that this man live two extra years beyond medical expectation, he would *not* have lived; however, had prayer failed to be offered and every effort made to fulfill the primary will of God for him, he might well have died prematurely. There was divine purpose in this extension of life, a purpose we cannot understand, yet I think of the many I have known whose lives have been prolonged far beyond medical possibility. In so many of these individuals I have seen an awe-inspiring spiritual growth.

I think in this connection of a woman with cancer. Had she died three years before she did, she would certainly have been spared much suffering, yet she grew from a nominal Christian to a spiritual giant in those three years. During the last hours of her life she asked her husband if she was dying. He replied, " Yes." She squeezed his hand and whispered, "These past three years have been the most glorious of all our lives together." With this her husband, who had watched her suffer and had suffered with her, concurred.

The mother of a twenty-year-old girl asks a question pertaining to her personal experience.

"Every time I prayed for Helen," she said, "I received the assurance that she would be all right. This impression was so strong that at times I was sure I heard a voice saying, 'Don't be afraid. Helen will be healed.' I claimed this promise," the mother continued, "but Helen was not healed. Why did I receive this assurance when, in fact, she was to die?"

This experience of assurance is not unique. Often the individual is healed here and now as we have prayed; sometimes the healing comes through death. In either case the assurance is valid, and our claim is honored. It is simply that we tend to forget that we are even now living in the midst of eternal life, that we are separated from our beloved dead by only the thinnest of veils—our physical senses. Thus we have mistaken the assurance because we make so vast a differentiation between life and death, when actually life is a continuum, beginning when we come from God, and continuing eternally when we return to Him.

The mother of this young girl asked the inevitable anguished question when the young die: "But why should she have died before she really lived?"

We don't know. Again, although we are certain that it is not God's perfect will that a young girl die of cancer, we cannot be sure that her death itself was not according to His purpose. Much prayer was offered for this beautiful young woman, who came regularly to healing services. We observed the increasing radiance about her and watched her grow in Christ to an awesome degree. Perhaps she died because of the unbelief of the world, the lack of faith of the church universal, our own imperfect prayers. But just perhaps she had fulfilled her purpose here on earth, for she touched and inspired countless lives in her own so-brief one. All of us who knew her grieved for her family and for ourselves; for her we could know only joy that she was now fully with her Lord, whom she so greatly loved.

One of the great joys of the healing ministry to me is that those who know the healing Christ are unafraid to die. They go to meet their Lord with joy, knowing that His *is* the "greatness, and the power, and the glory, and the victory" (I Chron. 29:11).

For those left behind, there is much suffering; but the anguish is eventually transcended by the triumphant knowledge that the one they love is now wholly with Christ, in whom lies the final victory.

Chapter 20

"WHOM SAY *YE* THAT I AM?"

A CERTAIN DAY stands out clearly in my memory, because within the space of a few short hours great truths of the healing ministry were capsulated.

It began on a Sunday morning when I had an appointment with a theologian who was coming from many miles away to discuss the ministry of healing. I had just returned from early church when the doorbell rang and I ushered in the distinguished-looking and very dignified middle-aged man with whom I was to spend the next three hours.

At the end of ten minutes of conversation I knew him to be a brilliant and immensely complicated individual. At the end of fifteen minutes it was evident that he had not in reality come to "discuss" the healing ministry, but to tell me his story and ask my advice and prayers for healing.

Some months before, he had undergone an extremely traumatic personal experience, which had led him into an interest in the ministry of healing, about which he had known virtually nothing until that time. When I saw him, he was in a state of great emotional conflict, and doubtless as a result of this had developed a severe physical disability. The latter, however, was the least of his concerns at the moment.

A scholar with an outstanding mind, he realized that his intellect was a stumbling block. He was aware that he lacked the simplicity of faith generally required of us if we are to receive the healing power of God.

As he talked, I listened carefully with my physical ears to what he said, and equally carefully with my spiritual ones for the guidance of the Holy Spirit. It was abundantly clear that God would have to be the counselor, not I, for from the human viewpoint his problem seemed insoluble.

He talked for over two hours, I said what I felt guided to say, and then we prepared for prayer and the laying on of hands. The entire situation was so complex that the man was unable to state precisely what he wanted prayer for, nor did I of myself have the remotest idea how to pray. With the supplication that the Holy Spirit pray in me according to God's will, we began. In the middle of the healing prayer, the presence of God was so overwhelming that I was forced to my knees. Necessarily removing my hands from his hand, I actually saw the hands of Christ replace mine. At that instant, the man began to pray in an undertone along with me. I was quite certain that he had never prayed in that manner before.

Suddenly laughter and joy, which seemed to emanate from the innermost depths of his being, began to erupt in this man. At the end of the prayer, he rose from his knees, thanking God, laughing and crying at the same time. Again and again, with what I sensed was for him unprecedented abandon, he exclaimed, "Praise God!" And then he said, "It is all so *simple*. At last I can see that He can take care of the entire situation. *He* is now in control, and there is nothing I have to do except praise and thank Him."

This man had a real conversion experience, and both he and the brokenness in his life were healed. As a corollary, his physical ailment had instantaneously disappeared.

His words, "It is all so simple," have stayed with me. Time and again I have emphasized that the healing ministry is not *easy*, for it is incredibly difficult for most of us to become again as little children. But *simple* it is, and this man, by the grace and touch of the Lord Jesus, had been able to discard his intellect, and becoming again as a little child, had been converted (Matt. 18:3). For the very first time, he knew what the joy of the Lord really meant; not because he had been healed, but because he had experienced God.

God is giving us—and the world—a choice. "Come unto Me," He says, "and you shall be endued with peace and power." Or, "Go your own way and destruction will be wrought—not by Me, as an act of vengeance—but by yourselves, who are voluntarily choosing the hell of your own making instead of the heaven of Mine."

Our choice depends upon our individual response to the question He asked of His disciples two thousand years ago and continues to ask of each of us today: "Whom say ye that I am?" (Matt. 16:15).

Many who before could not answer this question with certitude have come through the healing ministry to echo with grateful hearts the reply of Simon Peter: "Thou art the Christ, the Son of the living God" (Matt. 16:16), the Christ who cures the sick, heals all suffering, and binds up the wounds of the broken-hearted.

When we say and mean, "Thou art the Christ," we open our hearts to the love and enabling power of the living God within us. We open our hearts to the transcendent God, Who directs and rules our lives. We see

His hand in all the blessings of this life, both great and small.

"Whom say ye that I am?" The Christ, the Son of the living God; He who dwells in me and I in Him. He, as Saint Paul says, "who was crucified through weakness, yet liveth by the power of God" (II Cor. 13:4). He whose touch is upon me and my life; He who is responsible for everything I do which is good, for every breath I draw. He of whom I am somehow conscious every time I walk across the room; He who governs and plans my life if only I will listen and obey; He who forgives and loves, no matter how great my transgressions. He who guides my every faltering step along the road to holiness—that incredibly difficult path I could never travel alone. He who raises me each time I fall; He whose light shines in the darkness, illumining the narrow way I seek to tread and the strait gate that lies ahead. He who finally picks me up in the everlasting arms and carries me through, so that at the last I am wholly with Him whom I worship and adore and fervently long to praise and serve throughout eternity.

"Whom say ye that I am?"

Thou art the Christ, the Son of the living God; the Saviour of the world who by Thy Cross and Precious Blood hast redeemed and saved us.

This is the Christ whom I love beyond this world; the Christ who died for me; the Christ who carries my burdens, who suffers with me so that I am never alone. Thus the yoke of this life becomes easy and the burden light in Him.

"Whom say ye that I am?"

Thou art the Christ, the Son of the living God; the Lord of great pity and tender mercy (James 5:11), whose promises I have claimed, and so know that He is faithful.

"Whom say ye that I am?"

Thou art the Christ, the Son of the living God: Light of Light, Very God of Very God, of whose kingdom there shall be no end.

We have made our irrevocable choice; for "He who commanded the light to shine out of darkness, hath shined in our hearts, to give the light of the knowledge of the glory of God in the face of Jesus Christ" (II Cor. 4:6).

Afterword

To be a Christian is an exciting and wonderful thing, and I think we don't sufficently realize how immeasurably blessed are those of us who claim the Christian faith.

It is what we *are* (the fruits of which are how we live and what we do) that makes us Christians. And what we are is what God has made us to be by a special act and how we fulfill this act in our own lives. What is this act? According to the New Testament, it is incorporation into the human nature of Christ, by which His life is communicated to us. We are re-created in Him, for "if any man be in Christ, he is a new creature" (II Cor. 5:17).

As vital members of the Mystical Body, we are empowered by prayer and sacrament. As Saint Thomas Aquinas has said, these are the means by which we love God in act, so that the divine love may communicate itself to us, and through us, to the world. If we fail to take Christ, who is the embodiment of love, out into the world, we dare not call ourselves Christians; for it is only in giving Christ to others that we are able to possess Him ourselves.

The divine love can be communicated through us whether we are physically sick or well. I am only grateful that God upheld me when I had to stand, and endowed me with His supranatural strength so that I might keep working in His service according to His will.

My own physical healing is almost, though not entirely, completed. After nearly six years without one day free of pain, it is for me no small miracle to have now many pain-free days; to be able to have friends in for dinner once again; to take walks; to sit up and read until midnight. These are small things of themselves, perhaps, but each is a victory, together making possible a nearly normal life. Long after I am completely well, I shall see in the ability to live a normal, pain-free life a miracle never again to be taken for granted.

I shall always remember the past years with gratitude to God for His never-failing grace—grace received in many different ways, but for me most abundantly through the sacrament of holy communion, which is the supreme unitive experience of God upon which my life depends. As we partake of His Body and Blood and thus receive His life in us, we are made whole, regardless of suffering, by virtue of ourselves offered and Himself received. I am forever grateful to God for His mercy in answering those prayers uttered during countless sleepless nights that by morning I might be able to receive Him in whom lies all life.

I am grateful to God beyond the telling for His patient love in teaching me those things I could have learned in no other way. Among these, I have learned now, experientially, that it is through pain-filled eyes that we see most clearly the Christ who never forsakes us.

I understand, now experientially, the joy of the Christian who, though lacking all else, knows that His Redeemer lives, and that in Him there can never be despair.

I have experienced the love of God in a fuller way, as I have looked with new eyes on that love shining in all its glory through our Lord as He hung on the cross. I see now that He was impaled there not by the nails which pierced His hands and feet, but by the love He bore us all and lived and died to save.

I know now why it is that the fervency with which we embrace the cross determines the extent of our joy.

"These things," Jesus said, "have I spoken to you, that my joy might remain in you, and that your joy might be full" (John 15:11). I have heard "these things," taken them to myself, and my joy is indeed full.

Dare
To Live
Now!

Bruce Larson

GUIDEPOSTS ASSOCIATES, INC.

Carmel, New York

Bruce Larson's DARE TO LIVE NOW! effectively mirrors the author's fresh approach to Christianity and his extraordinary ability to draw out lay leadership. DARE TO LIVE NOW! is honest and provocative. It should prove a helpful guideline for individuals and small groups.

CATHERINE MARSHALL

INTRODUCTION

Jesus spoke a great deal about this present life and relatively little about our future life. His recurring message was, *"Now is the acceptable hour!"* and "The Kingdom of God is *at hand!"* This book is written in the belief that Jesus Christ can change life here and now for any individual, family, church, or group who will discover how to appropriate the power and love which are His.

The chapters in this book have been written over the past dozen years. Many have already appeared in print as articles, initially in *Faith at Work* Magazine. Each chapter deals with situations or circumstances in life that will be fairly common to most readers. It should also be said that the author does not see himself so much as a writer as he does a clinical observer and reporter of man's needs and God's intervention.

The reader will quickly discover that all of these chapters have a single purpose. That purpose is to be as concretely helpful as possible in presenting the *how* of faith in some of life's most basic situations. While it is true that there is an initial turning point in the life of every Christian, it is also true that there are daily turning points. It is in handling these that a Christian is effective or ineffective, victorious or defeated. The purpose of this book is to make clear at each turning point how a person can lay hold of God's willingness to help and to heal and to guide.

Each chapter of this book is highly personal and reveals much of the author's own search for wholeness, maturity, and integrity. I am grateful to the friends, parishioners, colleagues, and most especially family members who have patiently and lovingly and incisively been used of God in the turning points of my own life to date. Next to the gift of Christ's own friendship and presence, I thank Him most of all for the companions of the way whom He has sent.

BRUCE LARSON

New York City
December, 1965

Contents

1. | DARE TO LIVE NOW!

Man's Predicament and God's Challenge

LIFE IS MEANT to be an adventure. Thomas Carlyle said about someone, "He was born a man and died a grocer." Sin is not just breaking the law but failing to discover the adventure at the very heart of living.

I know a middle-aged man in Canada who for years carried a little black book in his pocket where he recorded all of the unloving and insensitive things that his wife had done to him over the years.

A tanned New York executive in the advertising field told me that he was retiring prematurely and wanted to spend the rest of his life in a lighthouse. He said, "For thirty years I have been coping with people and I have run out of cope."

A young woman who was devoted to God and who spent much of her time and service in the church and in serving others contracted an illness that kept her in bed for years. She described her condition as, "I couldn't die and I couldn't get well."

A gifted clergyman confided to me one day, "The other

night I woke up and saw my wife sleeping beside me and I realized that there was no way out of our hopeless relationship. Divorce is unthinkable and I don't see how either of us can change. I love her, but I don't know how to live with her."

At a funeral the widow told me that for years her husband slept with the lights on and a radio playing afraid to go to sleep lest he die. His doctor told this man, who weighed three hundred pounds, that unless he dieted his life was in danger. The more he feared death, the more he ate. He died at fifty-five.

A young man from Philadelphia, getting a divorce after three years of marriage, told me, "We thought we were meant for each other. Before we were married she'd go sailing with me and love it, and I used to enjoy going to hear her play in a string quartet. But now I get a headache whenever I hear chamber music and she gets seasick every time we go sailing."

A young suburban mother near Boston confided to a small group that in spite of having five children, "I am not a good mother. I find that I don't enjoy children, not even my own."

A six-foot teen-ager in a Canadian college told several of his roommates and friends, "It comes to me that I love my parents very much and appreciate greatly all they have done for me, but I've never told them so. And I know they love me, but they have never said so."

A New Jersey man in his thirties said, "I am so ashamed of the way I treat my family. Why can't I be the man at home that I want to be?"

An executive returned from a conference on creative relationships sponsored by his company and run by a team of social scientists. "The first question they asked us," he said, "was, 'Tell who you are, apart from your job or title.' I found that I was unable to answer and it scared me."

Who am I? Why do I do the things that I do? Why do

other people do what they do? Is God concerned about me and the trap I am in? If He is, what can He do to help me? These are the most basic questions of life.

In the fifth chapter of the book of John, we find a man trapped by life's circumstances. He had been ill for thirty-eight years and was looking for a cure. He spent his days beside a pool where the sick came from far and near. It was an authentic center of healing like Lourdes today or Ste. Anne de Beaupre or possibly was even the counterpart of one of our large medical clinics.

Jesus saw this place filled with human need. He walked among the patients and stopped beside this man who had been there for the greater part of his life and who had obviously been failed by the best medical and religious knowledge of his time. Jesus asks him an amazing question, "Do you *want* to be healed?" On the surface the question seems irrelevant and unfair. Of course this man wanted to be healed. He had spent most of his life in this place where healings occurred from time to time through the curative waters.

However, instead of a simple yes or no, he says, in essence, "Sir, I perceive by your question that you have entirely missed the point. My problem is that the people I have been counting on to put me into the pool at the right time never seem to show up. They are always late." How much this man sounds like a great many of us when asked about our condition. We say, "You see, it's not my fault. My mother was a neurotic. My father was seldom home. My employers have never appreciated me. My friends have let me down, and my wife doesn't understand me." There is something comfortable about the theory of "environmental conditioning" and even depth psychology that lets us off the hook. By blaming others for our present dilemmas we miss the very key to escape.

The issue as God encounters us in the midst of life's pressing situations is not man's goodness or worthiness, for who is worthy before God and who is good enough?

As Jesus intrudes on this man's life the real question is, does he want to pay the price of being well? Though illness may be a great inconvenience, it has many fringe benefits. Illness can be a way to escape the drudgery of work and the burden of responsibility. Each day this man would watch his friends and contemporaries going off to work in hot fields or stifling shops, while he could lie in the cool of the porch beside the pool and discuss the news of the day with his friends or passers-by.

When he was brought home each night, I'm sure this man got preferential treatment from his family. We all know families in which Father whispers to the children, "Let's not upset Mother; she has one of her migraines." By being ill we can often get our way with people who would resist us if we competed on an equal basis.

Self-indulgence can be another fringe benefit. Things that we would not condone in others, we can excuse in ourselves if we are ill, in pain, or incapacitated. Illness is also a way of getting attention, sympathy, or praise.

These suggest some of the things that may be involved in any illness. We can never assume that someone who is ill has an undivided desire to recover. Jesus simply asks this man if he dares to receive the gift of wholeness and begin to live and compete in the world on an equal basis. At some point in this dialogue (which is certainly not recorded in its entirety), the man by the pool must have answered "yes." He is healed, picks up his bedroll, and walks into a new way of life. How different his experience was from that of the woman hypochondriac who, when she died, had carved on her tombstone, "Now will you believe I was sick?"

In trying to understand the human predicament, we see, first, that all of us are being trapped by life in some hopeless situation that can stifle all joy and adventure and fulfillment. No one is immune. On the other hand, we believe in God's love for us, which is not conditioned by our goodness, and His power to release us and transform us. The basic question is, what are the things in us that prevent or block this healing and release?

An experience of mine during World War II has given me some helpful insights into our common predicament. I was a new infantry recruit at Fort Benning, Georgia. When I sat down to my first breakfast in the mess hall, with ten other men at a family style table, I saw something in a large bowl that looked like cream of wheat. I scooped up a large amount in a bowl and poured on milk and sugar. A tall mountain boy sitting across from me was bug-eyed and said, "Is that the way you eat grits?"

As a Chicago boy I had heard of grits but had never seen them before. Now I had learned something and filed it away for future reference. But rather than exhibit my ignorance, I smiled self-assuredly and said, "Oh yes, this is how we eat grits in Chicago." He was amazed as I finished the bowl, which tasted terrible. But I kept my eye on him and discovered that the proper way to eat grits is with butter and salt and pepper.

Some days later I happened to be sitting at the same table with this same rangy mountaineer. Grits again were served that morning and under his watchful eye I took a bowl, scooped up some grits and again poured on milk and sugar. Somehow I managed to eat the mess.

The whole tragedy of the human predicament is demonstrated in this incident. We do not want to admit our mistakes. We would rather go to hell maintaining our innocence than to say, "I was wrong." Specific confession of sin seems to be extremely difficult for most of us in life's situations. Many in psychiatric work maintain that emotional and mental illness is often caused by our insistence that we are right. By admitting some error of long standing, we move toward maturity and healing. God asks us, "Do you want to be healed of some emotional or moral or physical ailment or do you want healing in some relationship?" When we can reply, "Yes. I have been wrong, I want to make things right and begin again," Jesus challenges us to take up our bed and walk. It may mean asking forgiveness or a change of jobs or to start fresh in any number of costly ways.

Another factor in man's predicament is his desperate need for love. This perhaps underlies our defensiveness and refusal to admit error. Being made in the image of God, we are not like God, but made to need God and His love. We are meant for love and have an almost unlimited need. It is so important for us to be loved by family and friends and colleagues that we dare not reveal our imperfections lest we be rejected. This is the motivation behind self-righteousness and pretense. It is this need for love that makes us destroy the very people for whom we care the most.

When we lived in Illinois, I owned a dog named Jock. He was a miserable dog who destroyed my wife's rugs and the neighbor's shrubs and the nocturnal peace of the neighborhood. But he had one outstanding quality. He loved me deeply.

As I went to the church or the hospital or made calls, Jock used to follow my car and always arrived shortly after I did, much out of breath. I would pretend to be angry when I saw him coming and would always sternly rebuke him. But inwardly I would gloat and think, *I'll bet few people have a dog that loves them as much as mine loves me.*

All this time my wife kept saying a prophetic word, as wives have a way of doing. She pointed out that if Jock wasn't chained, or trained to stay at home, he would surely be run over some day. Some day came. He was not only run over but killed and I was the one who killed him! He caught up to me at a stop sign and, not knowing he was there, I ran over him.

There is certainly truth in the old song, "You Always Hurt the One You Love." But it wasn't my love for Jock that destroyed him. It was my great need for his love. As parents we destroy our children because we need them so much that we act not in their best interests but out of our need. Jesus Christ offers to give us a new Spirit to motivate us and control us. This Spirit does not need people in this destructive way, but makes it possible for them to act on the basis of others' needs, rather than their own.

I cannot change the things in me that are most destructive. The question is: Am I willing to be changed? This is God's business. When we put ourselves into His hands, willing to be made new, we find that He is not only able but eager. Such is His love!

The Canadian college student mentioned earlier did go home to his family and was able to tell his parents that he loved them. This opened up a whole new relationship where they, with tears in their eyes, could express their love for him. Parents and a teen-ager discovered a new dimension of life and communication. It began when a son experienced God's love and received a new Spirit and a new ability to love.

Some years ago God confronted a redcap at Grand Central Station who hated his job and all the menial and degrading aspects of it. When Ralston Young, Redcap 42, heard Jesus Christ's challenge, "Dare to live now," he responded. He thought he would be given a new job, but found that God did not intend to change the circumstances of his life. Instead, God, through this redcap, has performed one of the most amazing ministries of our time. Three times a week at noon there is a prayer meeting on Track 13 which has attracted thousands over the years. Lives have been changed and redirected, marriages healed, and problems solved. It began when one redcap accepted his environment and heredity and circumstances and responded to God's challenge for healing and newness. This redcap, at the heart of New York City, has learned how to love others in a redemptive way.

A beautiful young mother in the middle of a nervous breakdown was taken to a large hospital in St. Louis where she resisted all therapy. She was hurt that her husband and her mother would permit her to be confined to the psychiatric ward. For weeks she was sullen and morose and uncooperative.

One day she was standing by the barred windows of the ward looking out on Kings Highway which runs by the hospital. All of a sudden this woman, who had grown up in the church and knew the great truths about God, suddenly heard Him say to her, "Ruth, I love you. You don't have to live like this. Stop struggling and let me have your life and all of the resentments in you." When this awareness of God's love and Christ's presence came, something in her broke and she felt released. When she confided this to her doctor later that day, he told her that he saw an astonishing change. He called her husband and she was released the next day and went home to live a new life, with a new center and a new sense of her own worth.

God is trying to speak to us in all the circumstances of life. He wants to do more for us than merely relieve our pain or alter our circumstances or make life more comfortable. He is trying to show us the smallness of our own concerns and to demonstrate what His life in us can be if we give Him a chance.

Toward the end of World War II, in a Japanese concentration camp, the guards, learning of the imminent approach of the American army, unlocked the gates and fled to the woods. But the prisoners inside did not know this and remained in their cells. When the liberators came, they had only to announce to the prisoners that they were already free.

God has liberated all men through Jesus Christ. No one really has to be a prisoner of circumstances or environment. The good news is that we are *already free*. The message we announce to our friends is that freedom is available for all because of God's love and power in Jesus Christ. The only conditions seem to be that we admit we are prisoners and then risk leaving the security of old patterns and walk out into sunlight and freedom. It is not easy to live responsibly and in freedom and it is a challenge. Jesus says, "I came to bring release to the captives," and "I came that you might have life and have it abundantly." Dare to live now!

2. | WHAT IS YOUR NAME?

A New Name Can Make You a New Person

A COLLEGE STUDENT at a recent conference was asked, "What is the most meaningful thing that has happened to you recently?" His answer was surprising. "Let me tell you," he said. "Several weeks ago I had my handwriting analyzed and was told that I am an extrovert. I didn't know that. All my life I have been timid and shy, with a huge inferiority complex. But now that is all changed and I have been having a marvelous time these last few weeks!" And he wasn't fooling! A new name had given him the power to become a new person.

The Bible's story of Jacob and his twin brother Esau is as fascinating and contemporary as the children next door. Jacob was a mother's boy and his brother was an outdoorsman. Thus the seeds of life are sown!

The very name "Jacob" means "supplanter" or "cheat." Jacob cheated his brother. He cheated his father. He cheated his father-in-law. He lived up to his name. The turning point in his life came as he was leaving his father-in-law with two of his daughters for wives and half of his livestock secured by trickery. As Jacob traveled toward home, he learned that his brother was coming to meet him with a large force of men.

Such a setting is perfect for conversion. Jacob is the man who has been "adjusting" his income tax when word comes that the Bureau of Internal Revenue wants to look at his books. He is the man who has been cheating on his wife and discovers that someone has told her. He is the student who has been putting off studying all semester and then comes to exam time. Life has a way of bringing us up short. One day we all face who we are and what we have done to people.

Suddenly Jacob faced a lifetime of deceit in the imminent approach of Esau. The night before he was to meet his brother, who had every right to rob him or thrash him or kill him, he was ready to hear what God had to say. He sent his family and servants and cattle on ahead and waited by the brook of Jabok. There he met God and wrestled with Him all night. As dawn came, the Person with whom he wrestled said, "Let me go, for the dawn is coming!" (One cannot see the face of God and live.)

But Jacob said, "I will not let You go unless You bless me."

Here is the really strange thing. When God said to Jacob, "I will bless you," God went on to ask, "What is your name?"

"My name is Jacob" (or cheat).

And God said, "Your name is no longer Jacob. It is Israel. Cheat, you have become a prince. That is your real name."

And the amazing thing was that this man became a prince of God, the person for whom the Israelite nation is named, and for whom Christians are named because we are the new Israel. He was the spiritual founder of all that we cherish, both as Jews and Christians, because God called him by his rightful name and he became what he was called.

We find this happening all through the Bible. When a man is ready for a blessing, God often gives him a new name — Simon became Peter, and Saul became Paul.

In subtle ways we give each other names-within-names. And the devastating thing is we become what we are called. Each of my children has a particular name and knows exactly what I mean when I call out, "Christine!" "Peter!" or "Mark!" All too often the name means that they must be more careful about their things, pick up their rooms, return library books, improve their table manners, study harder, bathe more often, or treat each other more lovingly.

How Do You See Yourself? Is your name Timid, or Dishonest, or Self-conscious, or Fearful, or Indifferent, or Reserved? The name by which God calls you might be just the opposite. It may be that your real name is Courageous, or Faithful, or Warm, or Generous.

About a year ago I met a man at a clergy retreat. At the opening meeting tempers got out of hand. Many of us were somewhat edgy and ruffled. This particular man, though not one of the official leaders, was the person who again and again was God's catalyst to change the atmosphere. His humor and insight and honesty were refreshing.

The next morning at breakfast he walked by my table. I grabbed his hand as he went by and said, "Trevor, I want you to know that I thank God for you."

"Oh, Bruce," he said smilingly, "I thank God for myself!"

I was amazed. I thought, this explains it. He can love others because he loves himself. He has all the troubles we have and is not perfect, but he can love himself because he knows that Jesus Christ loves him and he dares to call himself "Beloved."

How Do You See Others? If the names we call ourselves determine who we are, do the names we call others determine who they become? I have seen this happen and have marveled at it.

We had a thumb-sucker in our family who finally got to first grade and still sucked his thumb. I was frantic and tried everything I knew to break him of the habit, including scoldings, arguments, prayer with him, prayer for him, and the vile-tasting things that are concocted to put on children's thumbs to deter them from this persistent habit. But he was unable to stop. I kept telling him that I was doing all this for his own good and he heartily agreed!

But one day I realized what my true motives were. I was really embarrassed to have my child advertising to the world the emotional needs of his own home and the inadequacy of his parents. I saw that my love for this child was conditioned by my need for him to stop this habit. When God showed me this, I made a new commitment of myself to Him and began to affirm what a truly wonderful son I had.

I stopped correcting, nagging, or even referring to the thumb-sucking in any way. God had set me free and I secretly called my son by a new name, "Mr. Wonderful." I didn't care if he ever stopped sucking his thumb. The miracle is that in ten days he stopped cold and hasn't sucked his thumb since.

People often behave the way they do because of a name we force on them. An employer, an employee, a son, a daughter, a husband, or a wife can be put in a box by the name we give consciously or unconsciously. But I know firsthand how the miracle of a new name works, for I have been on the receiving end too.

Last summer our family had planned a long automobile trip across the United States and Mexico and I grew panicky as the departure date grew near. I am a compulsively neat, fussy, meticulous person who should never have inflicted himself on a wife and children. I want everything clean and in its proper place. For me things tend to become more important than people. Persons like me make it awfully hard for others and while God has done a great deal to set me free from this condition, I was afraid that a twelve-thousand-mile trip with five people and a Springer spaniel in one car would undo it all. I did not want to spoil the trip of a lifetime for my family.

On the third day of our trip, as we were having breakfast with friends in Montgomery, Alabama, I said to our gracious hostess, "Louise, you and Sid better pray for me these next two months so I won't be a block to God. I am a real neurotic, you know, and need a daily miracle."

Mark (our seven-year-old), who was sitting next to me, said, "Daddy, what's a neurotic?"

"He is a crabby old man."

"Oh, Daddy, you're not crabby!"

I was all set to tell him to cut the flattery, when I looked into his eyes and saw that he meant what he said. I was struck dumb. Was it true that this little boy did not see me as a crabby daddy?

We had an amazing trip and I had only one really bad time during those eight weeks. (That's not a bad average for a neurotic!) And I think the turning point came when my young son called me by a new name. He saw me through Christ's eyes and saw who I really am. I became the person I always wanted to be!

After I had preached in a New York church last year, a lovely young woman came up and said, "You know, Bruce, God has really changed my life since the conference two months ago. I have been having a terrible time with my mother for several years. She and I share an apartment and we fight all the time. She is possessive and demanding and we just go at it. I have prayed and prayed but nothing ever happened. But God worked a miracle at the last conference.

"The change came when Don James (Director of the Pittsburgh Experiment) told a story about two psychiatrists with offices in the same building. They often rode up on the same elevator together in the morning. The one who got off first invariably turned around and spat on his colleague. The other would calmly pull out his handkerchief and wipe his face, tie, and suit before getting off a few floors later.

"One morning the elevator operator could contain his curiosity no longer. As he was closing the door on the first psychiatrist, he said, 'For heaven's sake, Doctor, tell me why your colleague always does this to you.' The second psychiatrist calmly replied, 'Oh, I don't know. That's *his* problem!'"

The young woman told me that this story made her realize that her mother's behavior was her own problem. "God wants me to love her just the way she is and try to make life fun for her. I have changed tremendously since I saw this and God has even begun to change her!"

As long as we pray for people as problems, we will have problems on our hands. If we pray for a nagging mother, we will always have a nagging mother. If we pray for an indifferent husband, that is exactly what we will have. But claiming a new name for another may open the door for a miracle.

How Do You See Situations? Situations, too, become what we call them. We can pray for a problem office or a problem school or a problem home and forget the Lordship of Christ over every circumstance. We don't take Jesus Christ into our office, school, neighborhood, or church. He is there already. He wants us to discover Him there and claim the place for Him.

The first time the Israelites came out of Egypt heading for Canaan, their spies reported, "We can't take the place. It's full of giants, large armies, and walled cities." The Israelites believed the spies and doubted God's promise, so God made them wait forty years and raised up a whole new generation. Then new spies went in and reported on the same situation — the same walled cities and the same large armies, "We can take this place because God has said so. The land is ours!"

Now, do we see a problem business or a problem school or neighborhood like that? Do we pray, "Lord, this is Your business I'm working in. Nobody here may know it but You and me. I may be only a janitor (or a clerk or secretary or salesman), but this is Your business because the whole world is Yours. Lord, I belong to You, so I claim this place for You."

I know a man who some years ago was a junior executive in a business. He had begun his Christian life by facing up to some failures in his marriage and family. After God began to work in his life by changing these basic relationships, he began to face his job. In a small fellowship group that met weekly for study and prayer, he said one night, "You know, I can't stay in my job. I'm being asked by my superiors to do things that are dishonest. I'm low man on the totem pole and I can't fight it. But as a Christian I can't be dishonest."

We all prayed and for nine months he looked for a new job. He would have taken half the salary just to get out of that situation. But after months of closed doors, he finally said to the group, "I think I'm supposed to stay where I am and let God change the business through me." Two weeks later a young salesman who had been one of the most irreligious and immoral men in the business invited him to attend his baptism. God had changed his life and these two men became a team. Once a week over lunch they met to pray for the business and for each of the office staff by name. Soon there were three men meeting for lunch to claim God's best for the business.

Although not a word was said to anyone, within a year the ethics, philosophy, and moral fiber of the company were so changed that none of the three was asked to do a dishonest thing. It all began when one man said, "Lord, I claim this place for You." Incidentally, this man is now a senior executive and the primary person responsible for setting company policy.

As Christians we believe that God loves us and that Jesus Christ is alive and in the world working for our good. We believe that He has all power and that He wishes to transform us and make us and our world new. Finding your real name or the real name of others may be the beginning of this miracle.

3.

ARE YOU FUN TO LIVE WITH?

The Acid Test

IN THE MIDDLE of our comfortable weekly luncheon meeting of Christian businessmen in midtown Manhattan, a Congregational minister from New England, Lee Whiston, dropped a bomb when he asked us, "Are you fun to live with?"

Most of the regular members of the group had from time to time confessed problems pertaining to their families. But with Lee's question, our traditional Christian concern for our families was shattered. Lee suggested that if we were living as Christ would have us, our families would enjoy living with us.

Well, we have never forgotten Lee's question, and each of us lives with it daily and refers to it in the group from time to time. God used that question to check my own motives and attitudes. Why do I want my wife or my children "to be more Christian" at times? Is it because I want God's best for them or because I want God to change some annoying trait in their lives that is creating a problem in mine? Is my motive really love — or am I using God to nag my family?

Several years ago when I had been having a faithful devotional time each morning (and my wife had not), I greeted her very irritably at the breakfast table. She had the Christian love to suggest that if this was all my "quiet time" was producing, maybe it would be better for me to spend the time in bed. Going to work on the bus that morning, I saw how I had been misusing that time in the morning, and was only feeding my self-righteousness. If I had really been spending time in God's presence, it would have made me a different person at the breakfast table.

The home is the most difficult — and rewarding — place for any Christian to put his faith to work. It's much easier to be effective and loving and faithful and gentle with people we only see from time to time. Unfortunately, we cannot fool the people who share our home. I am convinced that *we are what we are at home!*

Years ago I actually thought my family held me back spiritually. Now I see that God has given me at least one place where I can test how far I have come in this new life and relationship which He offers.

The home is the place where Christ can speak most clearly. I would rather hear God speak through almost anyone else than through my wife or my children. I can "take it" when He speaks through the minister, or through a friend, or through a book, or through His Word. But to recognize God speaking through my wife's loving rebuke or suggestion takes a great deal more grace. And if God is to speak clearly, whom can He better use than the one who sees me most clearly, loves me most unreservedly, and understands my needs most deeply?

At the heart of our Christian conviction is the belief that God wills newness of life, peace, joy, and love, not only for individuals, but for families. Here are four things we feel

God has been trying to show our family over the years, so that we can co-operate with His purpose and plan for us.

The first is the most difficult. *If you really want God to make your home new, you must let Him begin with you.* It is difficult for the member of the family, whether parent or child, who thinks he is "furthest along spiritually" to make the first move in a total surrender of his will and life to Christ. The instinctive thing is to hope that the others will catch up to us, so that we can "go all the way" together. This is never the case. One member of the family must be the spiritual pioneer and become totally vulnerable to the others in the family for Christ's sake to initiate God's action in a home.

I remember a couple who were married for nine years and who were living in hell. She claimed that he was romantically and emotionally cold and escaped from the home at every opportunity. She was involved in many civic and social and church organizations to find meaning for her life. Her husband, on the other hand, detested the kind of homemaking and cooking that his wife did (or rather did not do) and said that he could not feel warm toward someone who was so irresponsible in the home. Each declared that should the other change, he or she would follow suit.

One day the wife came to see me, on the verge of a divorce. I will never forget the miracle that began to happen when she promised God, on her knees, that she would be everything that her husband wanted her to be as a homemaker, for Christ's sake. She went home then, not out of a sense of duty but out of a new and deeper experience of God's love, and began to minister to her husband out of the fullness of that love. It took about a year for the husband to respond totally and to face up to the person God wanted to make of him as a husband.

Many of us live in a stalemate and cry, "Unfair! Unfair!" But the only way to break the stalemate is for one to go all the way. Each going halfway is never God's solution for a marriage.

There is an amazing verse in I Peter 3:1 that says, "You wives be submissive to your husbands so that some, though they do not obey the word, may be won without a word by the behavior of the wives." (That verse applies equally to husbands!) How wise the Apostle Peter was in sensing that we are not to talk about our faith at home, or if we do, to talk very sparingly. The thing that counts is to live a new and radiant life day by day and to be "fun to live with."

A second thing that our family must learn again and again is *how to love in God's way*. We are all aware of how children learn to manipulate their parents. They know how to "butter up" Father for an increase in allowance, the use of the car, or permission to do something usually forbidden. Unfortunately, most adults relate to each other in just the same way only with more sophistication.

When God's love captures us and we have the resources from within to live out the pattern for love described by the Apostle Paul in I Corinthians 13, we no longer have to manipulate people, but are free to be vulnerable to them and to their demands. This is what Christ meant in the great commandment to love one another as He has loved us. We have the promise that this kind of love never fails.

God's love working through us is permissive and unconditional. That means it is not conditioned by the response we get from people but by God's abundant supply in us. It offers freedom to others rather than rigidity. It is wrong to force family prayers or church attendance on an unwilling spouse or grown children. If Jesus Christ has truly made us new, we then have the resources to live so that they will *want* to pray and worship with us.

My wife and I laugh often at how we must continually learn to give love in terms meaningful to the other. Each of us would rather give love in the ways that we enjoy giving rather than in the ways the other enjoys receiving. How many hundreds of times in our fourteen years of marriage have I come home to a freshly baked pie. When God has spoken to her and convicted her of some failure in our relationship, she has often expressed her love or repentance by baking a pie. Now I don't especially like pie, but I have had to eat an awful lot of it in fourteen years!

In the same way, I have come home ready to hug and kiss and whisper sweet nothings to a spouse with whom I was most unloving or in violent disagreement a few hours earlier. At such times romance is the last thing that she wants from me!

We keep learning from God what to do after He has changed one of our hearts. We need to ask Him *how* to express this new love that we feel so that the other can receive it unmistakably. God wants to love people through us and He has to show us His unique strategy for loving each person He sends us.

One of my favorite contemporary theological works is the comic strip "Peanuts." Some months ago poor old Charlie Brown was coming home from a baseball game muttering, "One hundred and forty to nothing! . . . I just don't under-stand it! . . . And we were *so sincere!*" How often I have been sincere in expressing a new love God has given me for some-one at home or in the office or elsewhere, but my strategy was all wrong. We need more than sincerity and a change of heart. We need to let the Holy Spirit show us how He can get through us in ways that will be meaningful to those on the receiving end.

I received a great deal of help a few years ago from a small group we belonged to in Illinois. One couple was concerned about a pre-school daughter, their only child. The father, who was extremely busy in all manner of church, civic, and scouting activities, felt that he was so out of touch with his daughter that he would have to drop some worthwhile activities and spend more time with her. He tried this with no result. One night he came to the group excited. He told us that God had revealed to him that it was not more time that his daughter needed but *all of him* for a brief time each day. He had been aware that when he was playing games with her or reading to her or doing anything with her he always had part of his mind on something else, or was carrying on a conversation with his wife, or was watching T.V. His daughter never had more than half of him. She reacted to this (as all of us do) and had all the symptoms of being unloved and rejected.

When God showed this man that one of the ways to love is to give another one's undivided attention, the relationship with his daughter took on a new dimension. This same thing is true for husbands and wives, brothers and sisters, roommates and all others with whom we are in contact. I will always be grateful for this lesson. I have had to learn it again in each new relationship.

The third lesson our family is learning has to do with *total honesty*. Real communication between God and man or between man and man requires total honesty. Most of us hide behind our masks and pretend to be people we are not. How hungry our family is to know us as we really are and to be known as they really are.

Our children need to know of our past failures and what we did when we were their age. They also need to know of our present failures and where we need forgiveness today. If in our family prayers we can be honest about ourselves, we do more to introduce our children to God than in all of our prayers for them. As a matter of fact, we must do much more praying with them. (It is best to pray *for* them in our private devotions.) In marriage we need to open our hearts totally to a spouse and learn to say, "I am sorry" or "I was wrong" at the appropriate times.

What happens when our children see us lose our tempers, become unfair or unjust, and then kneel in family prayers with them and pray for all the missionaries around the world and the minister in the church and Aunt Martha and Uncle Jim? They know this is phony and is not really being honest with God at all. When we can include prayers for our present needs in their presence (of which they are all too aware), they will almost invariably respond to the reality of Christ themselves.

The main thing to remember is never to hesitate being honest about yourself, but always hesitate being honest about another.

I believe that God will show us how to say things to others about their needs in those rare times that require it. One Christmas morning I received a handsomely wrapped package from my youngest son, which turned out to be a bottle of deodorant. On the card were the words, "Not because you do. So that you won't!" What tact! I have often wished that when it did seem right to talk to someone else in the family about his needs, I could have the gift to say things that way.

As we meet in prayer and discussion groups, we need to be

honest about some of the desperate situations we get into as families. I remember sitting at lunch with a group in Ontario who were talking about marriage. One of the women, a charming person of early middle years, was telling about her own past and present difficulties with a problem husband (the only kind God makes!). Someone asked, "Did you ever think of divorce?" She replied with a perfectly blank face, "Divorce? No! Murder? Yes!"

We all laughed and from that point the conversation took an entirely different turn. We began to be honest about the cost of being God's people and discovering newness as husbands and wives together. That kind of honesty in any Christian group is a gift.

The final thing that I personally struggle most with is *letting others in the family minister to me*. As a clergyman, I have an idea that I must always be right and the source of all Christian truth. Christ tries to show me that He is in my home independently of me and that some of His greatest truths come not only from my wife but from my children, even the youngest. God is there and He is working and I must enjoy being on the receiving end as others are used by Christ to minister to me. I believe that I am becoming free of having to bring Christ to my family. I might add that it is a great deal more fun to discover Him already here in our midst.

However, the battle is not easy. About a year ago I was having a difficult relationship with a wonderful Christian man. He seemed to judge me and criticize me no matter what I did. One day he wrote me a letter. I was furious and brought it home to my wife. "How in the world can I answer this?" I grumbled and showed it to her. She made several suggestions that I disposed of quickly because I didn't think she understood the devious nature of this man's spirit.

Finally she turned to me and said, "Why don't you take the advice you're so free to give all the rest of us?" (I knew something was coming!)

"What is that?" I asked.

"Why don't you admit to God that you have no love in your heart for this man and ask Him to change you?"

"That's ridiculous!" I shouted, and stomped out of the room to read the evening paper until dinner was ready.

That night in saying prayers with my ten-year-old daughter, I no sooner got to my knees than I had to face what I knew God had been trying to say to me through my wife. I asked His forgiveness in my daughter's presence and asked God to change me. My daughter concluded her prayers by saying, "Lord, you know that Father is a difficult man to change, and yet we know You can do it, and I ask You to give him Your love for this man."

Now this is not the role I have chosen for myself. I would rather be the teacher, the prophet, and the authority in my home. But frankly, this does not always work, and lately I've begun to enjoy being a learner with my family at the feet of Jesus Christ.

I have been told that traditionally there are two schools of thought in Germany. The industrial, practical, northern part of the country has this philosophy: "The situation is serious but not hopeless." In the southern part of Germany, more romantic and perhaps less practical, the philosophy seems to be: "The situation is hopeless but not serious."

The latter certainly expresses the basic Christian attitude about life. Apart from Christ's love and presence in us there is not much hope for us and our families, being the people we are. But when we take the Gospel seriously and realize that Christ is with us and contending for us, we can then look at

the grimmest situation and say, "It's hopeless but not serious."
Jesus Christ is alive and loves us and wants to give us and our
families joy and love and newness of life!

4. LEARN TO LOVE

Life's Greatest Adventure

"LOVE IS THE MEDICINE for the sickness of the world," said Karl Menninger, one of the great contemporary figures in the field of medicine and psychiatry, some years ago.

Dr. Menninger told his staff, including doctors, nurses, orderlies, and cleaning people, that the most important thing they can offer a patient is love. For when people learn to give and receive love, they recover from most of their illnesses, whether physical or emotional. This is the secret behind the amazing success of the Menninger Clinic in Topeka, Kansas.

Other psychologists and psychiatrists are saying similar things. Erich Fromm believes that loneliness and the inability to love are the underlying causes of psychic and emotional disorders. Paul Tournier, the Swiss physician, talks of the need for persons to remove their masks and to discover and be discovered by other persons. Simple love and honest friendship can bring healing.

Hobart Mowrer, professor of clinical psychology at the

University of Illinois, denies the basic psychoanalytic theory that emotional illness results from a barrier between the conscious and the unconscious in a person. He believes emotional illness results from a barrier between the conscious self and other people. It is our inability to love and be loved, to have friends and be a friend in any depth, that causes much contemporary illness. When honesty and sharing of life begin, healing often begins.

Carl Rogers, founder of the famous nondirective school of counseling, says of persons that come to his University of Chicago school for training as psychotherapists that he can quickly train those who have what he apologetically calls "love." (He says there is no other word to describe the quality which makes a good counselor.) Without "love" no amount of training can make a man or a woman effective. And so the evidence mounts in medicine and psychology regarding the therapeutic need for love.

Moving to the political scene, many prophetic voices in government have spoken of the need for genuine love in America's foreign policy. This view has been wonderfully illustrated in the excellent book, *The Ugly American*, by Lederer and Burdick, which maintains that no give-away programs of material will really do the job in the world. The primary need is for love in the hearts of people who go out and administer our foreign policy. Our overseas ambassadors, whether for the State Department, the Peace Corps, or representatives of industry, must become rightly motivated. People respond to genuine love in other people — and to the lack of it.

While the underprivileged nations' most pressing needs are material and technical, their greatest need, as ours, is still for human love.

I recently spoke to a Swedish pastor who was visiting New

York. I asked him for the cause of the numerous teen-age gang riots in Sweden. He said that Sweden has achieved an almost perfect form of socialism where all material needs are effectively being met, but that the nation has forgotten how to help young people find a reason for living, a spiritual focus for life, and depth relationships. People still need more than medical care, material security, and peace to live life together successfully and creatively as individuals, families, or nations.

The communists are succeeding in winning neutral nations where we are failing, not because they genuinely love these nations but because they at least give the *appearance* of love. America, on the other hand, is like the rich uncle who enjoys giving gifts but not giving himself.

A veteran leader in foreign missions for the Presbyterian Church told me that when President Eisenhower visited Kabul, Afghanistan, not one of the 250 people in the American Embassy could translate the President's speech to the people. On the other hand, each one of the eighty employees of the Russian Embassy, including the chauffeurs, was able to speak the language. This gives some indication of the tragic lack of identification which has so often characterized our foreign affairs. We can be thankful that we are learning from our mistakes.

In other corners of the human arena the same plea is heard. There is a desperate suppressed cry for love coming from the works of the successful novelists and playwrights of Europe and America. Whether we read Albert Camus, Tennessee Williams, Françoise Sagan, or a host of others, or analyze many of the current plays and films, we are overwhelmed with the recurrent theme of loneliness and separation.

Our world is becoming increasingly aware of the need for love, both on the international scene and in the back wards of mental hospitals. Christ is calling His Church in this age to love people with His love in all the common affairs of daily life.

What is this love that the world is looking for? Christians know that God is love. Love is not a technique that can be learned; it is a gift. Erich Fromm says that when we need someone it is impossible truly to love him. He defines mature love as, "I love you, therefore I need you," rather than "I need you, therefore I love you." There is a profound difference. God needs us because He loves us, and when His love enters into us through Jesus Christ, we need people because we love them. The person who has not experienced this love of God must of necessity love others only because he needs them. Then true love is impossible.

Love does not have to prove itself. Much of our service to others in life comes because of an awareness that we do not love a person as we should and therefore must prove our love to him and to ourselves. This is why over-generous and non-disciplining parents betray the fact that they do not love their children enough. I know of one couple who insisted on taking an old father into their home when he would have been much better off in a place where he could have received nursing care and quiet. They had to prove to themselves and to him how much they loved him. When they finally saw how little real love they had for him, and prayed for a new kind of love, they were able to release the old gentleman to a different kind of life where both he and they were much happier.

Basically we know when we are loved with a divine love. When someone comes into our life filled with Christ's love, we respond to the divine in him. I know a woman who discovered this new way of love. She was on the visitation committee in her Episcopal church and brought altar flowers to shut-ins. One gruff old parishioner at the hospital said to his minister, "Tell that girl who was here Sunday that she can keep her blasted flowers but to come back. Something happened to me while she was here." This love is so different from anything the world knows that we never have to wonder if we are giving or receiving it.

Love is God's greatest weapon. When a living Christ can enter a human life and begin to act and move through it, everything changes. Two or three high-school students in one large city carried on a quiet war of love against a harsh, unfair, irritable teacher. Instead of reacting to her, which would have been natural, they began quietly to love her and secretly to pray for her in the classroom. She was in time transformed, and the entire class and school felt the impact. Illustrations could be given from every kind of life situation regarding the power of love to transform people and relationships.

How can Christians learn to love this way? Four basic principles can help us. The first two have to do with receiving Christ's love; the second two with transmitting His love to others.

First we must believe Christ loves us *just as we are*. We are impatient, grumpy, irritable, nagging, fault-finding at home or in the office or in school because we really hate ourselves. It is difficult to believe that right now, in the light of what we have just done, God loves us as much as He says He does. When I find myself critical of people I live with at home or work, I don't need more patience but time alone to let God remind me of His love for me. When I know that I am loved by Him and am forgiven for present failures, then I find the things that have been so irritating in my family members or colleagues become trivial. We must learn to take the Cross seriously and experience day by day and moment by moment

Christ's overpowering love and forgiveness, not only for sins past, but for sins present. He does not say to us, "Change, that I might love you." As we read the Biblical record of Jesus talking with people, we sense His total love for them as they are. This love motivates them to change. We do not repent *in order* to be loved, but *because* we are loved by Him.

Secondly, we must be ourselves at all times. "If the Son shall make you free, you shall be free indeed." We must not repress feelings that are wrong but let them come out where God can deal with them. We tend to think that being a Christian is to pretend love for those whom we do not love and smile meekly to hide the churnings inside. "Telling somebody off" may not be the Christian way, but it is certainly healthier than pretending nothing is wrong.

We Christians have a wonderful promise, "For there is therefore now no condemnation for those who are in Christ Jesus. . . ." We must be ourselves, believing that Christ loves us as we are and does not condemn us. "If we confess our sins, He is faithful and just to forgive us our sins. . . ."

In transmitting this love to others, the first principle is to let *others* be themselves. We must learn that it is not our job to change other people. Our job is to love them or to let God change us so that we *can* love them.

One of the most amazing centers of Christian love I know is Hidden Springs in Brantford, Ontario. Here a group of Christians are helping people adjust to life. One of the questions they keep asking their patients is, "Do you want to be right or do you want to be well?" When we stop having to prove to ourselves and to others that we are right, we have come a great way in learning how to transmit love.

We must learn not to take people at face value. We have to go beyond their faces to their hearts. Many people who smilingly tell us that they are, "Fine! Fine!" are crying inside and are desperately lonely and confused, looking for someone in whom to confide. If we can be sensitive to people, we give them a chance to be themselves with us. If we can let them know we understand something of disappointment and sorrow and guilt, perhaps they can then tell us of their real feelings and of the "impossible" turn life may have just taken.

Secondly, we channel the love of Christ to others by believing in Christ's love for every person we meet. Perhaps this is the most revolutionary principle of all. Christ does not ask us to feel loving toward everyone we meet. This is impossible when someone has offended us or wounded us or done something unfair or dishonest. But we can believe that He loves that person at the very moment we are seething with resentment. We are asked to use our wills to let go of our resentment and to allow His love to come through us. It doesn't matter how we feel about that person as long as we are willing to be a channel of God's love to him. This is an entirely different thing from trying to generate love or trying to change our feelings. We must learn to live above the level of feelings. By faith we can be a link between Christ and the person in need.

Frank Laubach has provided many with perhaps the most concrete way of opening the channel. He suggests that we throw one arm up vertically to receive Christ's love and throw the other arm out horizontally to channel it. We receive Christ's love with one arm and aim it with the other.

If we are in a situation where this is physically impossible, we can do this, "one arm up and one arm out," mentally. Over and over again I have seen God not only change my feelings in a moment but actually transform the person to whom I have been a channel.

The greatest adventure in life is to experience the love of God in Jesus Christ and to transmit it to others. As Christians we must be clear about what this involves in every situation, to fulfill the mission that He has given us, "This I command you, to love one another as I have loved you."

5. PERSON TO PERSON

The Secret of Effective Communication

I HAVE A FRIEND who is extremely self-conscious. When he comes into a room where there are small children, he tries to ignore them, hiding behind a newspaper or book, or becoming absorbed in television. But invariably the children, whether they are his relatives or total strangers, climb all over him and refuse to leave him alone, even though he says, "Go away and stop bothering me." Children are not put off by his gruff exterior. They know that it hides a warm and genuine love.

On the other hand, these same children will sometimes run from a sweet old lady who says, "Come here, Dear, and give Auntie a big kiss." They know that inside she is no lover of little children and possibly no lover of anyone but herself.

People respond more to how we feel about them than to what we say to them. For years Dr. John Casteel has been saying to students at Union Theological Seminary in New York that dynamic Christian truth is transmitted *relationally* rather than *propositionally*, though he concedes that it is often a difficult truth for seminary students to comprehend, since their focus is so much on the theological content of the Bible.

Because I am fascinated by the way life-changing truth is communicated from person to person, I have recently been conducting an experiment. I have asked literally hundreds of people, in small groups and individually, two questions. The first is, "What single person has had the greatest influence on your life?" The replies have always been illuminating, both to me and to the people who have answered the question. Very few have pointed to such obvious people as parents or ministers. The persons most often mentioned are grade-school teachers or high-school teachers, older friends, distant relatives (frequently a grandparent), or a much older neighbor or Sunday school teacher.

The second question has been even more illuminating. I have asked them to describe the nature of their relationship with this person. Here are some of the significant characteristics of these dynamic relationships.

Identification. "The person who most influenced me treated me as an equal," is often said. The person was in some superior role, either because of age or experience or status. The important thing was that he did not use that superior position as a platform from which to help, but was able to stand alongside the other. Remember how Jesus washed the feet of the disciples and told us to do the same! D. T. Niles, of Ceylon, says that the Christian Church often misses the mark because we Christians would rather *give a service than be a servant.* The servant identifies with the person he is serving and is willing to be a subordinate. There is a vast difference between this and bringing another a service he needs, whether it be food, medicine, teaching, or counseling!

A few months ago a woman told several of us about a prayer and study group she had organized in her suburban neighborhood. For months this lovely woman had tried to help the "lost" in her neighborhood, but with little success. The group seemed hopeless. One morning she had a rare fight with her husband and the group was to meet that afternoon. At first she thought she would have to stay away. When she finally went, she broke down and told of what had happened, and concluded by saying, "I have no right to teach you. I shouldn't even be here in this condition!" Then guilt overwhelmed her and she left hurriedly. She was afraid that she had completely lost her effectiveness, only to find later that three of the young housewives made tremendous spiritual advances that day because their teacher had demonstrated that she was "one of them." If she was really like them *in their needs*, they concluded, they wanted to know her Lord!

Listening. "He was always interested in hearing about my problems and my ideas," is another description of this influential friend. We mistakenly think that our knowledge or insight is the greatest gift we can give to others. Often we bring them much further when we eagerly listen to what they are trying to say about themselves and their problems. We affirm their worth and dignity by taking them seriously.

It is illuminating to study Jesus' way with individuals. He often got a "case history." Jesus would draw out the demon-possessed, or those sick or in trouble, by asking the person what he understood of his own problem. The Holy Spirit may do more to convict a person out of his own mouth by what he says to a loving listener than by all of the good advice and insight that may come from the mouth of another.

Personal Honesty. "He let me know what his own problems and needs were," is another description I often hear. One hears a great deal of concern expressed that religion can become "too personal." But Jesus did not practice secrecy about Himself. The only way we could know about His temptations in the wilderness is that He must have told His disciples, for no one else was there with Him.

Paul Tournier, the eminent Swiss physician, has contributed much to the field of counseling and psychotherapy along this line. Dr. Tournier is successful because he is honest about himself with his patients and does not relate merely as a professional person to a client. He relates as a person to a person. It is amazing how God uses this to build therapeutic relationships.

One evening as a men's group was meeting in our office in New York, a man came in whom no one knew. Each thought that he had been referred by someone else in the circle, and so it was suggested he pull up a chair and join the six or eight men who were meeting for fellowship and prayer. He sat and listened as several individuals talked about present struggles toward becoming whole people and effective Christians.

Finally the leader turned to the stranger and asked who he was. "My name is Paul," he said, "and as long as you have been honest, I will be honest too. I am a dope addict. I came here to rob this office to get a fix, but I think I have found something better." Paul stayed to pray and asked God for help with his serious problem simply because he heard some other men being honest.

Vulnerability. "He trusted me" is another answer I often hear. We need to trust others in costly ways even as Jesus trusted Judas, not only with His money but with His reputation and His life. This is one of Jesus' supreme messages for us and He commands us to love one another as He has loved us.

The night before this chapter was written, my wife and I

had dinner with a young couple who have in recent years discovered the reality of Jesus Christ. For some time we have known of their "experiment of faith." The wife began first by making a personal moral inventory and then praying with another person. Her three biggest problems had been her relationship to a daughter who was severely handicapped, a frustrated ambition to be a professional singer, and a husband who was fast becoming an alcoholic.

The morning after this prayer her husband woke up with a dreadful hangover. Without saying a word of reproach, his wife began to rub his back. He describes this startling change in her, which is still going on, as the incident that finally brought him to a surrender of his own life to Jesus Christ some months later.

To lay one's life down for another while he is confused and rebellious is hardly possible apart from the presence of God. How afraid we are that the other will take advantage of us if we don't preach to him and moralize with him about his problems. I recently had an effective Christian tell me that one of the secrets of his life is, "Never let another person's sins bother you until they bother him." If we really live this out, we will become involved with people in a costly way.

Willingness To Receive. "This person would often ask me to help him or pray for him," is another frequent answer. Jesus frequently initiated a new relationship by asking for help. He was never reluctant to ask for food or lodging or water or even company in His loneliness and temptation. This was His first step in graciously opening other lives for the help they needed from Him. We need to discover how to receive help from others, so that they may then accept what God may want to give them through us. As one friend of mine often says, "Don't be a stingy receiver."

Several years ago, I became suddenly ill at a conference in Bloomington, Illinois. I had all the usual symptoms that go with the flu, including chills and fever. I took to my bed in the men's dormitory. Within the space of one hour, six different people heard about my need and came to offer help. One anointed me with oil for healing — my first experience of it! Another knelt and offered prayer. The third person was a woman doctor who came in and gave me some aspirin, took my pulse, and reassured me that, in all probability, I had a twenty-four-hour flu bug. The fourth person brought me a tray of food, which was the last thing in the world I wanted at that time! The fifth just expressed concern, while the sixth, a wonderful Finnish masseuse, came in and sang hymns in Finnish while she gave me a massage.

Two things happened. First, I was healed within the hour. I don't know which one of those people was the channel of God's healing, but I suspect they all were used. But second, and even more exciting, I became aware that God was trying to teach me how important it is to receive help from Him through others. It is much easier for me to give than to receive, which has often been a block in relationships. I still thank God for that lesson and am grateful for my six "teachers."

So God communicates His life through us to others. The apostolic succession of New Life from person to person is a twentieth century reality unbroken since Pentecost.

6. | YOU AND YOUR JOB

Bringing Your Faith to Work

HOW DO YOU SEE YOUR JOB? Whether you are a homemaker, a student, or a factory worker, the attitude you have about your work reveals a great deal about your faith. The Bible indicates that every Christian ought to feel a sense of vocation in his work. If you are miserable or bored in your work, or dread going to it, then God is speaking to you. He either wants to change the job you are in or — more likely — He wants to change *you*.

Remember the story about the blind man whom Jesus healed? After our Lord touched his eyes, He asked the man what he saw. He reported that he saw "men as trees walking." When he had received a second touch from the Master, he saw men clearly. I suspect that many of us need a "second touch" by Christ to see our jobs in their right perspective.

A friend in Illinois had joined a small group of seekers meeting for prayer and Bible study and the sharing of their faith each week. Although he had come a long way in his Christian commitment, each week he complained about the customers in his store — how unfair they were, how demanding, and how they took advantage of him.

But one day this man received a "second touch" by God and began to see the people who came into his store, whether to buy a package of nails or a washing machine, as people sent by God. He anticipated each sale as an adventure in personal relationships.

At Christmas time, with all the rush of increased sales, this man said to the group one night in amazement, "You know, what surprises me is how the people in this town have changed. Last Christmas they were rude, pushy, and demanding, but this year I haven't had a difficult customer in my store! Everyone is understanding and trying his best to co-operate." They all laughed. They knew the change had not been in the town but in the storekeeper.

But in a more profound way, perhaps the change was also in the town. As we see people through the eyes of faith, they actually do change. They respond to us almost directly in proportion to the amount of love we have for them as people.

Let me suggest five questions each of us should periodically ask ourselves about our job.

(1) *Why am I here in this job?* Do you feel you are in your present job because of an accident? Because you happened to answer an ad, or your brother-in-law got tired of having you sit around and found you a job? Because of ambition? These attitudes certainly undercut any sense of Christian vocation. We should feel we are in our work because God has called us to it, in just as real a way as He has called any bishop, clergyman, or priest.

Several months ago a man asked me to call on him in his large office in New York City. He said, "A year ago I turned my life over to Jesus Christ. It happened in my church." He then described the change that had begun to happen in his home — new communication between him and his wife; deeper understanding of his teen-age daughter. There were many other evidences of his new commitment.

Then he said, "I find now, a year later, that I am still behind the same desk doing the same job in the same way, and I suspect something is wrong. If Christ has come in as Lord of my life, things ought to be very different in what I do eight or ten hours a day." He was right, of course. Now he is exploring, along with some other men, the opportunities and strategy for Christian ministry in daily work.

We must dispense with the myth that commitment to Christ means becoming a clergyman or that work done inside a church building or in a church organization is more holy, somehow, than work done in the market place. Christ came to give us a sense of calling in everyday work. This is where the world is changed, and where the Kingdom is built.

Jesus Himself was a working man, and He called twelve working men to be His initial disciples. He could have been born into a priestly family, but He was not. We must understand the really radical thing God has done in Jesus Christ, in wanting to build a new world and a new Kingdom primarily through committed working men.

(2) *For whom am I working?* Are you working for God, or for men? You cannot really serve both. When we are addicted to people's praise and thanks and rewards, we are in a real way under the tyranny of men and are working for them.

Often I feel terribly sorry for the wives and mothers in the world who work such long hours and never seem to be finished with their chores. If they are working for the appreciation and thanks of their families, they seldom or never get it. But when we work for God, we are free to serve others no matter how unreasonable or thankless they may be. Our reward is God Himself saying to us, "Well done, good and faithful servant."

Daily chores take on new meaning when we work for God rather than men. One woman has this inscription over her kitchen sink: "Divine services held here three times daily." What a marvelous freedom in washing greasy pots and pans, not for those who eat from them, but for a Lord who puts a woman into a home to serve a family for Him!

We need continually to ask ourselves whether we are willing to risk our jobs and our financial security in obedience to Jesus Christ. When we really work for God, and know that it is He to whom we are responsible, and from whom we get our reward, we are then free to be His people in any given situation.

(3) *What am I working for?* Wages? Prestige? Or am I working to do the will of God? This has much to say about our motives.

Christ's own life gives us a key. When He found people abusing others in the temple, He came in and violently upset the status quo. But when people wished to destroy *Him,* He let them drive nails into His hands. Perhaps this is the kind of freedom Christian men and women need in their jobs; not to protect their own interests, but to look to the interests of others; to protest when innocent people are being hurt, but not to protest for self-preservation. This freedom comes only when we can answer the question, "What am I working for?" with "To do the will of God."

Where is your security? Is it in the person who pays your salary or do you see him only as an agent whom God at this time has chosen to supply your needs? You cannot really love your boss or paymaster until you see him as God's agent. If you see him as your provider, then you cannot be honest with him, and fear and resentment are bound to color your relationship.

I have a wonderful Chinese friend, Moses Chow. His father was one of two sons in a family in pre-communist China. He had become a Christian and was told by his father that if he persisted in following this "new god," he would be disinherited.

There was wealth in the family, but Moses' father could choose only where he had found life, and life abundant. So, in his determination to follow Jesus Christ, he was disinherited and left China.

Moses Chow told us that his father went on to make a new home in a new country in the Far East, and has been quite successful as a Christian businessman. He left the security of the world and trusted God, who was able to provide. Meanwhile, Moses' grandfather and others fell victim to communism and lost everything. We don't follow God *because* He makes us secure, but our security is in God — even in economic matters.

(4) *With whom am I working?* God wants us always to be aware of the people next to us. It's not enough just to work honestly and industriously, for Christ calls us to be a priesthood of believers who willingly take responsibility for those who are our neighbors.

A railroad engineer came to his minister and asked to be put to work as a new Christian. The minister told the engineer that there was no position in the church open at the present time, but that there was a job, and it involved the question, "Is your fireman a Christian?"

This is the concept of the priesthood of believers, when we see that our primary job is not to be an elder, deacon, or vestryman in the church, but to be a priest to the man next to us in our daily work. This is where we need to recapture the marvelous vision God has for the priesthood of the laity.

God calls the laity to do a job the clergy cannot do in many instances. In a parish I once served, a close friend who was a doctor became quite ill. Though I visited him almost daily, I saw no improvement and no benefit from my visits. One day I went to see this Christian doctor and found him greatly improved and free from fear.

I asked him what had happened, and he told me of a visit he had had a few hours before from one of the senior surgeons in the area who had prayed with him and given him a prescription. The prescription was to read Joshua 1:9. My friend had been visibly touched by God, and not through a clergyman but through a brother physician.

(5) *What kind of place am I in?* Jesus Christ, by His very call to accept Him as Lord and Saviour, has brought us inside a revolutionary movement, so that the place we are in assumes tremendous importance.

No job is too menial to be of importance to a communist! Shouldn't this same thing be true for any Christian trying to build a worldwide Kingdom? Even a chambermaid making beds in a hotel can influence guests who go out and make decisions of worldwide importance. Christians should ask God to show them the nature of the place they are in. How important is the particular store, shop, industry, or service which is theirs? What could God do through that particular organization to change His world?

Recently I was speaking with a Congregational minister in New England. He told me of meeting with a group of high school students who wanted to know how to live their faith more effectively. He asked them to think hypothetically what they would do in their school if they were communists.

They brainstormed for a time and came up with a number of things they could do to sabotage the school: cut classes, sow discord, obstruct education in all kinds of ways, from telling lies to smoking in the basement.

Suddenly, one of the boys said, "Wait a minute, isn't this just what we are doing now!" It was a wonderful eye-opener for these young people to begin to see their high school as a place where Christ could begin to change the world through them. Later on they began to discuss just what it meant to be Christ's people, building a Kingdom in their own school.

There is a revolution going on in the world. Jesus Christ Himself is the leader, and when we accept Him as our Lord, He calls us into it with Him. He needs us. He wants us to see our jobs with the eyes of faith and understanding as something far more than a means of earning a livelihood. Our jobs are places where, as revolutionaries, we help to accomplish His revolution in the hearts and lives of men everywhere.

7. | DISCOVERING A CHRISTIAN MARRIAGE

Seven Words Unlock the Door

A FINE YOUNG ENGINEER I know, in the process of discovering a Christian marriage, said, "Marriage is wonderful, but it doesn't solve any of your problems." It is not supposed to! If you are unhappy before you marry, you will certainly be unhappy after you marry. Two people combine their problems when they marry, and living becomes even more complicated.

Christians believe that God intends marriage to be a wonderful, satisfying, and joyful relationship and that He has the power to make it so. And yet a truly happy marriage is not a common thing. Most of the marriages that fail never reach the divorce court.

We are surprised when a marriage "suddenly" breaks down. We are like the middle-aged man who began to lose his hair. Finally he had only one hair left on his head. He faithfully oiled and massaged that single hair. One morning he got out of bed and there on the pillow lay his one hair. With great anguish he cried out, "Great Scott. I'm bald!"

Marriage does not fail because one of the partners suddenly finds someone else who is more interesting. It is *because* the marriage relationship had already broken down that one of the partners began to look elsewhere.

No change in our circumstances is going to solve the basic problem in our marriage. A better house, more money, moving away from the "in-laws," or being able to have children will not really change a thing. We must become aware of the underlying causes of unhappiness that drive our partners to infidelity or alcohol or any of a hundred kinds of escape.

What is a Christian marriage? Basically it means that I can no longer do as I please. In too many marriages one or both partners do just exactly as they please and wonder why things aren't better.

This self-will can take many forms. It can be expressed as hostility. We resort to nagging or irritability or actual fighting with our spouse. Being afraid to face the genuine cause of a failing marriage, we choose certain areas for battle. We fight about where to squeeze the toothpaste tube, how to discipline the children, who spends the most money foolishly, why the house is not better kept, and whose habits make them "just like" their mother. Such fights give us a chance to express our hostility without getting into the deeper and more painful issues.

It ought to be said at this point that, when there is open hostility, we can assume there is still caring. The situation is more serious when a husband or wife does not even care enough to fight or get angry, and instead says, "You go your way and I'll go mine." In such a marriage a man recently told me that his wife seemed more like a college roommate.

When God is allowed into the lives of one or both of the people in a marriage, we see that the cause of unhappiness is within the individual. It is the feeling that we are not appreciated enough, that we give more love than we receive.

I talked with a couple recently about their marriage. The wife said, "But I always give in. I wish just once *he* would give in. If he loved me as much as I love him, *he would*." This is the basic frustration in all unhappy marriages.

It has been said that when two people marry, they become one, but the question often is, which one? Visualize two solar systems trying to occupy the same space at the same time; two suns vying for center with planets orbiting around each. The result would be chaos and collision. The same is true of a home with conflicting centers and different interests whirling around each. In some homes such a situation is solved by everyone yielding center place to one. Then the home centers around the mother or father or a child. Peace reigns, but the price is frustration and humiliation. This kind of peace is not the Christian answer.

In Christian marriage Christ is the center, and husband, wife, and children can find their proper orbit around Him.

Let us express this mathematically. In a marriage without Jesus Christ, 1 plus 1 equals 2. Where there are children, 1 plus 1 plus 1 plus 1 equals 4, and four centers in a home are hell!

The Bible says about marriage, "These two shall become one." Mathematically this means that 1 plus 1 equals 1. This sounds ridiculous in the science of mathematics, but it makes wonderful sense in the metaphysics of matrimony!

One attractive young couple came to realize that their budget was their biggest problem. Each felt that their tight budget and growing debts were the result of the other's irresponsibility and poor management. The subject was explosive and neither dared bring it up knowing the violent consequences. The wife expressed her rebellion by going on a periodic clothes buying spree, while the husband bought model trains.

When they admitted as new Christians that Christ could help them decide how they should spend their income, they were able in a short time to discuss their finances without anger, live within their income, and slowly begin to come out of debt. They set a time each week to go over the budget, and to remind them who had the final word, they always placed an empty chair at the head of the table.

Human love presupposes marriage to one's ideal. As disillusionment comes, the marriage breaks down. Christian love is not blind, but it has its eyes wide open. It does not vanish when the other's faults appear. A Christian marriage involves seeing and understanding the other person as he really is and loving him just that way.

Christ's plan for two people who are married and who live their lives in Him is that the wonderful glow of the courtship and honeymoon will not only last but deepen. True romance may not begin until we find this plan.

I can think of a couple married thirty years who are discovering Christian marriage after a lifetime of bickering and fighting. Today they are living in the glow of what it means truly to love each other. They are grandparents and also have young children of their own who share this new love in the home.

It all began with a conversation in which the wife expressed her life-long complaint. Her husband was hard to live with and touchy. He sulked and was unreasonable. He was extremely stubborn. Above all, *she* was active in her church and her husband was not. She wanted to know how to make her husband a Christian!

It was pointed out that if she were really a Christian, her only obligation was to make her husband happy, not good. This was a new thought. She saw that in spite of all of her church work, perhaps she had never let Jesus Christ become the center in her life.

One day she made a list of all the things she knew should be different in her life. Then she prayed, asking God to come into her life and change all these things. She discovered a wonderful new peace.

Five days later her husband, amazed by the wonderful change that had come over his wife, asked if the same thing could happen to him. He honestly faced the things that were wrong in his life and he prayed, asking Christ to forgive him and to change him and to take over his life. The marriage was transformed.

There is no way for God to change a marriage and leave the people involved unchanged. C. S. Lewis has said, "No clever arrangement of bad eggs ever made a good omelet." We waste too many of our prayers praying for the other person to change, when some really honest prayer for ourselves may do wonders.

Not long ago a woman came to her minister, begging him to tell her what to do with her alcoholic husband. She had taken all the abuse and humiliation and poverty she felt she could stand as the result of his drinking. Her minister asked her what she had done to try to change him. She said she had begged him, argued with him, shamed him, preached at him, read the Bible to him, threatened him, and prayed for him for years.

"Have any of these seemed to work?" the minister asked.
"No!" said the woman. "They have not."
"There is one thing you haven't tried. Why don't you pray

for *yourself*, instead of your husband, and ask God to change all the things in your life that you know are wrong?"

The woman tried it and it worked. Her husband stopped drinking. He no longer had to escape.

Anyone can discover a Christian marriage who will sincerely pray the prayer, "Lord, change this marriage beginning with *me*."

8.   PRIMING
        THE PUMP

Three Essentials of a Life of Faith

THE FOLLOWING LETTER was found in a baking powder can wired to the handle of an old pump that offered the only hope of drinking water on a very long and seldom-used trail across the Amargosa Desert:

"This pump is all right as of June 1932. I put a new sucker washer into it and it ought to last five years. But the washer dries out and the pump has got to be primed. Under the white rock I buried a bottle of water, out of the sun and cork end up. There's enough water in it to prime the pump, but not if you drink some first. Pour about one fourth and let her soak to wet the leather. Then pour in the rest medium fast and pump like crazy. You'll git water. The well has never run dry. Have faith. When you git watered up, fill the bottle and put it back like you found it for the next feller.

(signed) Desert Pete

"P.S. Don't go drinking up the water first. Prime the pump with it and you'll git all you can hold."

Nowhere have I seen the principles of faith more clearly set forth. What a person would do coming along that trail, half dead from lack of water and with an empty canteen would reveal much about his faith. Faith is not so much an academic subject for discussion or a theological term from the Bible, as it is something on which our very life hinges.

Faith is composed of three ingredients. First, there must be an object. It is impossible just "to have faith." If you were a lonely traveler coming down that parched desert trail, you would have to trust in an unknown person named Desert Pete to keep from drinking the bottle of buried water. This would not be easy. He is a person you do not know. There is a great deal of evidence he is telling the truth, but there is no guarantee that he is not a practical joker or a lunatic. So, the first ingredient of faith is trust in someone or something, based on evidence but not infallible proof.

The second ingredient is risk. Faith is always costly. If you were walking down that trail without water, there would be nothing more precious to you in all the world than a bottle of water. Desert Pete tells you that if you drink any part of that bottle of water he has left, you won't get any from the pump. So, it is necessary to risk the very stuff on which your life may depend to get a safe and sufficient amount. Faith is always expensive.

The third ingredient is work. Some people have mistakenly interpreted faith as a substitute for work. Faith is not laziness. Desert Pete reminds us that after we trust and risk, we have to pump hard!

Everyone uses faith daily. You have to trust either a partner in marriage or in business. Sometimes that trust is misplaced. In business, money and reputation are risked; in marriage, your whole life. For success, both a business and a marriage require a tremendous amount of work and consecration by both parties.

So much for faith. But what about Christian faith? This is no different in its ingredients. First of all, one has to have faith in God and especially in the way God has revealed Himself to man in the person of Jesus Christ. It is not faith in a principle but faith in a person — the Person!

Second there is commitment that involves risk. A total commitment always has specific and immediate implications that involve risk. It may mean asking forgiveness of another, making a specific restitution, beginning to tithe, or changing jobs. The more we commit of ourselves to God in very specific terms, the better we can know Him and His plan for our lives.

Third, there is hard work. After one has had faith in God and committed his life to Him, then comes the hard work. Some people have interpreted the Christian faith as just a matter of hard work. This leads to a kind of living which may be religious, but is not necessarily Christian. Christian faith is more than hard work for Christ and His Kingdom. But I have never known an effective Christian who was lazy.

In the Bible, Abraham has been called the Father of the Faithful. Because of his faith in God he left his home in Ur of the Chaldees. By faith he gave up the known and the familiar for the unknown and unfamiliar. He committed his life and his family and all of his possessions to the leadership of God, who called him to a new life in a new land. To find that new land and the new life required years of hard work. All of the men and women of faith in the Bible have had similar experiences.

How do we practice Christian faith today? The rules are the same. First we must believe that God is. Then we must listen to Him. When God speaks, we must obey every order we get, and it usually requires a great deal of faith and hard work. If we trust Him, God will do for us those things we cannot do for ourselves. But he will not do for us those things that we can do!

Many people wonder how they can know God's will. It really is not difficult. If we want to know God's will and are willing to do it, not knowing what it is, we have the assurance that He will make it known to us. Abraham Lincoln said, "When the Almighty wants me to do something in particular, He has a way of letting me know it." God *wants* to speak to us!

I know a fine young man, the father of four children, who recently began to put his Christian faith to work in his job. He is a manufacturer's representative for a large plumbing and heating firm.

One day he told me that a product he was selling did not measure up to specifications. He felt that, as a Christian, he couldn't sell a product he knew was dishonestly advertised. He knew God had been speaking to Him. However, he was certain he would lose his job if he refused to sell this particular product. We prayed about it, and he told God he was willing to obey.

I saw Dave a few days later. He had spoken to the directors of the company he was representing and told them he was convinced that the product was not all it was advertised to be and that he, as a Christian, could not sell it.

The result of this act of faith came some weeks later. The company withdrew the product from its line, planning to work on it and make it what they had advertised. Dave was commended for his integrity and retained his position. But it might not have turned out so well. There is no guarantee. If we could be sure of the outcome, faith would not be necessary.

Nicholas Murray Butler says, "I divide the world into three classes — the few who make things happen; the many who watch things happen; and the overwhelming majority who have no notion of what happens."

We all want to belong to that class of people who "make things happen." There is a desperate need today for people of Christian faith — people who will make things happen by God's power, according to His will.

9. THE SIMPLICITY OF PRAYER

How To Pray

JESUS SAYS QUITE SIMPLY, "*Whatever* you ask in my name, I will do it." How many praying people really believe this? All too many pray with the same faith one has in a slot machine, "It won't cost too much, and I might hit the jackpot."

I am convinced that most of us really want to know how to pray. We want to discover the power of God, which is rightfully ours in Jesus Christ.

Prayer is conversation between two persons. Now conversation in itself is neither good nor bad. We all know what it is like to talk to The Gossip, The Bore, or The Crank. Such conversation is not helpful and at times is really harmful. Then there is the conversation that you have with the man who comes to read your water meter which is neither helpful nor harmful but polite routine. Conversation is what you make it. It can be irrelevant, or crucial, as in a midnight phone call to the doctor. It can be dull or stimulating. It can

be necessary and business-like or it can lead to deep relationships in friendship or even marriage.

In the same way prayer can be as meaningless as much of
our conversation, or it can be conversation between you and
God that is vital, exciting, and transforming.

Conversation always implies a relationship between two
or more persons. The quality of the conversation depends on
the kind of relationship that exists between the two. This can
be as impersonal as that between you and the voice that
answers the phone when you dial "O," or it can be as intimate
as the relationship between a husband and wife.

As Christians our prayers should be intimate conversations
with God, because through Jesus Christ we become children
and God becomes a loving father. And yet, how many sincere
people wake up every morning, meet God at the breakfast
table, and say some little jingle that rhymes to thank Him
for the food. If you spoke that way to your husband or wife
every morning, it would be grounds for divorce. It would be
an insult to speak that way to an intelligent person.

Yet God, though He is a Spirit, is a Person. Why talk to
Him as though He were a statue or a simple-minded child?
This is why Jesus warns us, "Do not use vain repetitions (or
empty phrases) as the heathen do; for they think that they
will be heard for their many words." You deny that God
is your Father when you talk to Him only in memorized
prayers or little sing-song jingles. A child's first words to his
earthly parents are not a sing-song jingle, but a meaningful
word or two conveying an honest request. Why should this
not apply when speaking to one's heavenly Parent? When a
child is old enough to be taught to pray, he is old enough to
learn that prayer is merely conversation with a heavenly
Father.

What does Jesus mean when He says, "Whatever you ask in my name, I will do it . . ."? He does not mean to pray using His name as a sign-off at the end of a prayer, but rather to pray in His name by experiencing Him as Lord and Saviour and through Him to experience God as Father. Believing that God exists is not the same as experiencing Him as Father. To experience Him is to enter into a new relationship with Him Person-to-person and to grow daily in this relationship.

The most important single factor in effective prayer is that the person praying be in the right relationship with God. How does one enter this right relationship? I can put it quite simply in three steps:

(1) Take an honest look at yourself. Admit that no matter how hard you try, you never do become the person you know God wants you to be.

(2) Give up the hopeless job of trying to remake your life. Believe that God came into the world in Jesus Christ just to help you become the person you ought to be and, down deep in your heart, would really like to be. In Jesus we not only see God's love for us, but in the living Christ we experience the power to change that God makes available to us now.

(3) Put yourself completely in God's hands. Surrender to Him not only your problems but also your most cherished plans for the future. Don't hold back a thing. Believe that by seeking first His Kingdom, all that you really need shall be given to you.

Guideposts for Effective Prayer. Once you are in the right relationship with God, the following guideposts will prove helpful in making your prayer life more effective:

With Whom Should I Pray? Part of your prayer life should

include prayer alone with God. Jesus said, "When you pray, go into your room and shut the door and pray to your Father who is in secret." Part of your prayer life should be with others. Jesus said, "If two of you agree on earth about anything they ask, it will be done for them by my Father in heaven. For where two or three are gathered in my name, there am I in the midst of them." Pray as a family. How else will your children learn to pray?

When Should I Pray? Pray in the morning. Give God your day and your troubles and put yourself at His disposal for service. Pray in the evening. Take an inventory of your day and then ask forgiveness where you failed and thank Him where He gave you power to overcome. Pray all day long — while working or walking or talking with others. Learn to pray short sentences all day long that ask for help or give thanks. Let God know that you know that He is there.

In What Position Should I Pray? Pray on your knees in the morning and at night. There is nothing magical about the position. It is just that it reminds you with whom you are talking when you are sleepy and your mind may wander. Pray in any position throughout the day. The main thing is that you pray. The position is not important. I have one friend who talks with God while driving to work in the morning. He imagines that God is sitting on the seat next to him and they talk about plans for the day.

Listen When You Pray. At least half of good conversation ought to be listening. Most of us ask God for advice and guidance and then never listen for an answer. Spend half of your prayer time in quiet listening. Learn to expect answers. Believe that God really wants to talk to you.

Respond Immediately to Guidance. Respond immediately to whatever guidance God gives you in prayer. Until you walk in the light of what you have, you will never get more light. God's guidance is like the light on a miner's hat which throws a beam six feet ahead. Unless you walk those six feet, you will never see more of the path before you. So God's guidance is step by step.

When Praying for Healing. When you are praying for someone who is sick, know that God does not send sickness. Believe that God wants to heal the person for whom you are praying. Assume this when you pray! Don't keep saying, "If it be Your will" in your prayers for healing of a person. Of course it is always implied in all your prayers. But pray believing that God loves that person more than you do and wants to make him well.

Be Positive When You Pray. Be positive when you pray, especially when praying for someone who is sick. Have a picture in your mind of that person already made well and whole and ask God to accomplish just that. This is where faith comes in. Faith is not a negative attitude where you cry out to God to prevent the worst from happening (and hence carry a picture of that person at his worst in your mind while you pray). Rather, faith is believing that God will heal and has already healed through the presence and power of Christ, even while you pray.

Pray Believing. Jesus says, "Therefore I tell you, whatever you ask in prayer, believe that you receive it and you will." This is what faith is. It is belief in the love and power of God to act. Jesus says in another place, "Whatever you ask in prayer, you will receive if you have faith."

Relax. Relax, both physically and spiritually, when you pray. One man says, "Don't pray hard. Pray easy. Prayer doesn't do it. God does it." Relaxed prayer takes faith. Faith is demonstrated by our trust. Our trust shows in our relaxation. A good technique to follow is to pray with your palms open and turned up, not with your fingers clenched together. Lift people and situations and yourself to God for help on your open palms.

Surrender. Surrender when you pray. Don't merely ask God for help. Give situations and people to God and trust Him. This underlies all prayer and is the most important single guidepost to remember. It is not enough to believe that God loves us and can help us. We must so trust Him that we let go of things and give them to Him.

There is a young mother I know whose little boy of five came down with meningitis. She stayed by his bed in the hospital, helping the nurses and praying constantly, but his fever of 106° continued. After more than thirty hours a nurse said that with the medication he was getting he should have responded in five to eight hours. She implied that there was no hope. With this, the mother got to her knees and surrendered the child to God, whom she knew loved him even more than she did. As his pain was unbearable, she put Bobby in God's hands and asked Him for quick death or quick recovery, believing that this was what a loving Father would want for His child. As she surrendered him to God's love, peace came to her instantly. But that is not all. Within the hour the boy's fever broke and healing came.

Sometimes it is easier to surrender another than to surrender one's self. Catherine Marshall, in the book *A Man Called Peter*, tells of being ill with tuberculosis. At first she rebelled and asked God, "Why?" Then in the long months that followed, as she read the New Testament accounts of Jesus' healing, she believed He was alive and with her and that the same power was still His. She prayed for healing but nothing happened. Finally she realized that she was not surrendered to God. She put herself completely in His hands, saying that she believed He could heal her if He wanted to, but that she was willing to be an invalid the rest of her life if that were how He could best use her. Immediately upon surrendering herself to God, the X-rays showed that she was recovering.

Believe these three simple facts when you pray and you can expect miracles:

(1) Believe that Christ loves you even more than you love yourself. The Cross is proof of this. (Read John 15:13.)

(2) Believe that all power is His, physically as well as spiritually. (Read Matthew 28:18.)

(3) Believe that He is right there with you when you pray. (Read Matthew 28:20.)

Build your prayers on these facts, and then your Lord says to you, "Whatever you ask in My name, I will do it."

10. "WHERE TWO OR THREE ARE GATHERED..."

The Power of Praying Together

THERE IS NOTHING intrinsically good about praying or beginning a prayer group. Prayers and prayer groups are what we make them, or what we let God make them.

A prayer group can be as much an escape from the real issues of life as a cocktail party. Jesus may be calling us to face certain facts, or to make right certain relationships, while we escape Him and His demands by busying ourselves with a cozy group of Christians who enjoy being together, praying for the world.

A prayer group can be another burden to an already full schedule of activities, that, far from giving life, crushes the life we have and makes living even more fragmented. A prayer group can be as irrelevant as reading an old telephone book, or as out of date as last year's Christmas card list. Prayer can be offered repeatedly for the same people and situations. This is a denial of faith. There is something wrong about praying for the same things for the same people over and over.

However, a prayer group can be the most relevant, vital, powerful, and up-to-date appointment we keep all week. Through a prayer group that is open to God, lives can be changed and the whole course of human events altered. That this has happened many times in the past is history. There is no magic in just praying. Prayer doesn't change things. God changes things.

A prayer group must be organic to be vital. The organizational part of its life should be kept to a minimum. The best way to begin a family is to start with two people. Some of the most powerful prayer groups have begun with just two people meeting together for months, sometimes years, before growth. One recent group I know began when a minister and a newspaper editor promised God to begin a prayer group the next morning at seven o'clock. That night two additional men had their lives changed by God and the group doubled before it had met once. However, it all began with two men.

We should not be alarmed when our group has "ups and downs," for life has an ebb and flow. An organization may never vary. Most church committees are like the Bureau of Internal Revenue, that goes on and on with never a variation even though the personnel changes. You can build a house but not a tree. Life cannot be regimented.

The actual time spent in praying in a group is not the important thing. The real issue is not how long our prayers are, but how *real* they are — how *honest* they are — and how *much of ourselves* is in them.

Sometimes you hear the comment, "Our prayer group drifted into a Bible study." Now, none of us ever does enough Bible study, but it is wrong when Bible study squeezes out prayer and a relationship in depth with each other. Perhaps this shows a fundamental weakness in most of us in the Western world. We are more content-centered than we are life-centered. The East is concerned about "being truth," while we in the West are more concerned about "knowing truth." Jesus said, "I came that ye might have life," and the goal of both Bible study and prayer is Christ's life in us, not ideas about Him.

How we invite people to our prayer group reveals a great deal about what our group actually is. If we merely invite them to come and pray with us, we exclude all but those persons who seem to have a natural affinity for prayer. How many of Jesus' disciples enjoyed praying before He called them? It was the people with an affinity for prayer who crucified Jesus. The "needy" received Him gladly.

Prayer should never be the center of a prayer group. The true center is Jesus Christ and people's needs. Prayer is merely a link between the need and the answer. We should invite people to come and discover some answers for the needs in their own lives. Everyone has needs, and can be intrigued, especially if he has heard something from some of the members of the group about recent answers to their own needs.

Here are four points that will help make prayer alive in any prayer group:

(1) Prayer should be *realistic*. Christ's presence in a vital prayer group should make each person more aware of his own need for change, rather than the need for others to change. In almost every situation we are like the man complaining to the landlord about the noisy tenants upstairs who often stamped on the floor and shouted until after midnight. When asked if they bothered him, he replied, "No, I usually

stay up and practice the tuba until about that time every night, anyway."

Prayer should be realistic also in that we realize that changing our circumstances will not answer our problems. A new house and furniture will not change a marriage. Money to pay off a mortgage will not give life to a church. Health alone will not make a person happy.

(2) Prayer must be *honest*. We need to learn that God is not so concerned with our saying the "right" things as with our saying the "real" things. It was a turning point in my own life when I came to see that God did not expect me to say certain things in prayer, but rather waited for me to express my needs, even rebellion against Him, so that He could deal with me.

A young man was about to drop out of seminary. His devotional life had withered. He prayed only when he led worship occasionally in a little church. He was afraid to pray because he could not say the things he thought he ought to say to God honestly. When he discovered that God wanted him to pray about his lack of faith, his coldness of heart, his disinterest in prayer, a new relationship with God began.

(3) Prayer should be as *natural* as conversation, even though reverent. God is not stuffy and certainly does not want us to be stuffy with Him. Being formal and having a broken and a contrite heart are two different things. The language of prayer can be from the prayer book, but it can also be conversational. It is not how we pray, but what we pray about and the actual surrender to God of the things for which we pray that make the difference.

(4) Finally, we should develop a sense of *expectancy* as we pray. Hopeless prayers are the most pathetic things in the world. Real faith is expressed in expectancy.

When two or three are gathered together honestly, realistically, naturally, and expectantly, Christ can work miracles that heal cancers, heal homes, remove barriers, or bring spiritual awakening that touches countless lives. Anything is possible!

11. WHAT MAKES THE DIFFERENCE?

Honesty Is the Only Policy

GOD IS NOT SHOCKED by our sins. There isn't a sin that any of us has committed, or is now practicing, that Jesus Christ did not deal with realistically in His life and sacrificially on the Cross. Jesus associated with call-girls, alcoholics, and chiselers. He didn't condone what they did. Nor did He leave them as He found them. But the record indicates that they enjoyed His company.

However, it is recorded in the fifth chapter of the Book of Acts that two very fine people — Ananias and Sapphira — dropped dead in His first church. They weren't drunks. As far as we know, he wasn't stepping out on her. They went to prayer meetings. They were more than tithers. But they were pretending something that wasn't true before God and His people. They didn't have to give a cent from the land they sold to the church, but they *pretended* to give it all when they actually gave only half.

Now God didn't kill them. The spiritual laws are such that when we are hypocrites, we cut ourselves off from the life God wants to give, and often we pick our own kind of death — a sudden coronary, as they might have had, or some slow death. But death is inevitable, whether physical, mental, psychic, or spiritual.

How accurate a picture do Ananias and Sapphira give us of our own lives and our own churches? Do I dare find out who I really am? Have I let anyone else know who I really am? The lie we live is probably only a lie we tell ourselves. Most people who get close to us surely see more than we think but are too polite to tell us what they see.

The neighborhood bar is possibly the best counterfeit there is to the fellowship Christ wants to give His Church. It's an imitation, dispensing liquor instead of grace, escape rather than reality, but it is a permissive, accepting, and inclusive fellowship. It is unshockable. It is democratic. You can tell people secrets and they usually don't tell others or even want to. The bar flourishes not because most people are alcoholics, but because God has put into the human heart the desire to know and be known, to love and be loved, and so many seek a counterfeit at the price of a few beers.

Christ wants His Church to be unshockable, democratic, permissive — a fellowship where people can come in and say, "I'm sunk!" "I'm beat!" "I've had it!" Alcoholics Anonymous has this quality. Our churches too often miss it.

The rebirth of a Biblical theology in most of the major denominations today has resulted in a commitment-centered message. I genuinely rejoice in it, but it's not enough. One more altar call, decision card, church officers' retreat, or campfire surrender won't do it. Something else is needed. *A fellowship must exist where committed people can begin to be honest with one another and discover the dimension of apostolic fellowship.*

It is interesting to see that a large portion of the secular, indifferent, irreligious part of our society today often has more reality and genuine concern for others than many church people.

There is a minimum of soul-stifling pretense on the part of many pagans. They cheat on their income tax and laugh about it on the golf course. They get drunk in front of their whole club. They tell their marital troubles in detail to their hairdresser. They talk honestly to their bartender; they talk deeply to their psychiatrist; and they talk indiscreetly in the locker room to each other. But there is a real openness and transparency that is healthy.

We all know what can happen when one of these open, honest pagans comes to a Billy Graham meeting or some similar place and there is a chance "to make a decision." When the statement, "Jesus Christ, take my whole life," is coupled with their honesty, we see them born in the Spirit right before our very eyes!

Commitment alone does not open the door for the Holy Spirit to empower us and to do His desired work in us. A second key is needed. We can call it "honesty" — a word seldom found in a theological word book or concordance. The Biblical word "confession" makes most Protestants today think of a little booth and a priest. This is not what the New Testament writers intended. They meant people being honest with God in the presence of others — and being honest with each other.

For the committed Christian who has missed the power of the Holy Spirit to become a new person, honesty with another about himself can remove the blocks and bring freedom and release. The Holy Spirit will come in, do His work, and give His gifts. He does not have to be coaxed or implored. When we make the conditions right and remove the blocks, He is immediately free to heal and help and empower.

When God has His way and we are liberated, we know it and the world knows it. He doesn't make us perfect. We still have to say "forgive me" daily. But we "walk in the light" with God, each other, and ourselves.

Honesty is essential to Christian growth. God keeps showing me that at heart I am a phony (another name for a sinner). I used to tell out-and-out "social" lies, but I have gotten beyond that (restitution was too painful!). I am much more subtle now. I can lie with the truth. I can project an image which is all based on fact, but which gives a totally false picture about me, my family, my work, or my church. But when we live the honest, open life in apostolic fellowship, God's people puncture those lies. It is costly, but therapeutic and liberating.

Honesty is God's way for a family of Christians to become a Christian family. In our first church, after graduating from seminary, my wife and I were both committed Christians, but we hadn't yet discovered a Christian marriage. Two other young married women began to meet with my wife — both members of our church. Over coffee one morning the three admitted for the first time how they were failing as wives and mothers. When they prayed together, Christ's healing began.

We three husbands saw and experienced this change in our wives and soon there were six committed people living in honest fellowship, meeting together each week. The group began to grow and divide. Inside of two years there were about a dozen groups like it meeting throughout the city, involving people from dozens of churches. But it all began when three girls over coffee said, "This is who I really am. I don't want to be like this any more. Jesus Christ, will You change me?"

Our children need to know who their parents really are. This gives them freedom to minister to us. One of our sons, when he was six, prayed one night at family devotions, "Lord, forgive us for running all over the country telling people about Jesus and then being so grumpy at home!" They pray for us and become an instrument of Christ's healing. Their faith then is in Jesus Christ Himself, not in a false picture of their parents' goodness.

Honesty is also the key to fellowship. The equation for New Testament Christianity is fourfold. "And they continued steadfast in the apostles' doctrine and fellowship, the breaking of bread and prayers" (Acts 2:42). Most churches are strong on doctrine, prayers, and communion. But the apostolic fellowship is missing. This isn't the only way to the renewal of the Church, but it's part of the whole pattern. A three-wheeled wagon can't go far. All four wheels are required for the church to be the Church.

Honesty is the key to personal effectiveness. God uses my confessed, redeemed sins more than all the theology and psychology I've learned. When I'm counseling just with sound Biblical theology, I never see "Biblical" results. The price needs to be paid in personal honesty.

The Bible is full of the theology of confession. It begins with Adam and runs through the institution of the Levitical priesthood, the experience of the Psalmist, the conviction of the prophets, and on into the New Testament. Even church history tells us that the Early Church practiced confession within the fellowship for the first four hundred years. Confession to a priest became an option, and remained an option from the fifth century until a Papal decree in the thirteenth century made it the only way. With the Protestant Reformation confession to God alone became the only way for many.

Today with the renewal of the Church centering in rediscovery of the lay ministry and small group fellowship, we are about to see on a large scale new facets of the old truth that honesty is the *only* policy.

12. THE CHURCH IN REVOLUTION

God's Strategy for Today

AN ENGLISH BISHOP once said, "Everywhere Paul went there was a revolution, but everywhere I go they serve tea." We Christians are called "to turn the world upside down," but too often we end up confessing our oneness with this bishop. God is doing new things in our time and we who want to be effective must not be afraid to follow Him down paths that may seem strange.

Over 2500 years ago the prophet Isaiah reported God as saying, "Remember not the former things nor consider the things of old. Behold, I am doing a new thing; now it springs forth. Do you not perceive it?"

God does not change. The heart and mind of God are eternal. Rebellion and loneliness in the heart of man remain the same in all ages. But God's strategy in the world changes from one generation to another, conditioned by the times, the places, the events, the culture, and all the variables of human life. Many different facets of God's strategy for today have been observed and reported in the last few years. Let us look at a few.

A New Understanding of the Church. God is giving us a fresh understanding of the nature and the mission of His Church. In our time the Church has grown large and become prosperous. We know how to win members, raise budgets, erect buildings, organize and administrate effectively. But if the Church exists for the world, our very success undermines our mission and becomes an impediment.

We used to see the Church primarily as the clergy, with laymen helping with the chores, so that the clergy could get on to preaching the Gospel, helping people, making pronouncements, and attacking social evils. Now we see that laymen are God's primary instruments for helping individuals, for witnessing to the Gospel, and for attacking the forces of evil, while we clergy are to be their teachers and helpers.

If the Church exists for the world, and if laymen are the Church, then we in the Church need to experiment with new strategy. One church in California recruited fifteen of its most able men and assigned one clergyman to train these men intensively for two years. They were to be ordained as elders with the sole function of ministering outside the church — in the apartment buildings or neighborhoods where they lived, and in the factories and office buildings where they worked — with no teaching or organizational assignment in the church. When the Church thrusts its best men into the world in such a way even at the cost of weakening its own leadership, we see revolutionary Christianity. Churches, as well as individuals, must learn to lose their lives.

A New Strategy. Beginning with the Middle Ages, Christianity was thought of in terms of "Christendom," with the hope that the growing forces of Jesus Christ would gradually overcome the world numerically. But today the percentage of Christians in the world is actually shrinking and with it our whole concept of Christendom.

God is showing us again His original strategy, which comes with such newness in our day, that in Jesus Christ we are called to be leaven in society, not a massive force. We see here the wisdom of God, for *the revolutionary minority always has the advantage.* The strategy of infiltration is more effective than that of frontal attack.

There is a striking account in *The Ugly American* of an Asian country which had been occupied and controlled by the communists. A Roman Catholic priest from America gathered a dozen local Christians around him, and they began to meet secretly in the jungle to pray and think through a strategy of infiltration. In a very short time, God enabled them to overthrow the communist grip on their country and to produce an election that changed the government.

We need to see that two or three people in a neighborhood, or a dozen in a town, who pray and discuss strategy, can be God's agents for accomplishing His work in that place.

In a central Florida town there are two large neighboring churches. When the civil rights issue became crucial two years ago, one minister forced through an official statement of nondiscrimination against the will of his officers and members. The other minister resisted the pressure to produce a statement, but he quietly began to bring integrated groups into his church for conferences and meetings. To this day the first church has never had a Negro in it, though the pastor has been praised for his public stand, while the second has moved consistently over the last two years toward greater integration. To the latter, getting the job done was more important than wearing a hero's medal.

A New Center of Healing. The Church today is redis-
covering its authority for healing — physical, emotional, and
spiritual. Training in medicine and psychotherapy is important, but in addition to this we need communities of faith
and love where people are cared for deeply. Local churches
can and should be these communities.

I know of two rehabilitation centers, manned by relatively
untrained laymen, that are channels of God's healing for the
sick and emotionally disturbed. And I have personally seen
people who were not helped by individual therapy who were
brought to health through involvement with a small group of
laymen meeting each week.

I recently asked a professor of clinical psychology what
was the essential ingredient in training an effective therapist.
"Oh, that's easy," he said. "The people who become effective
are those whose lives are transparent to their patients." And
then he added sadly, "But we don't know how to put this
quality of openness and transparency into the people who
come for training."

The Church needs to move with boldness into this area, to
take responsibility for the emotionally disturbed, and to raise
up small groups whose members are willing to learn to love
and care deeply for one another.

At a recent conference in Oregon, a lovely young mother
stood up at the closing meeting to ask forgiveness of another
team member. "This is the first time that I have asked any-
body's forgiveness since I was seven years old," she confessed,
and turning to her husband asked, "Isn't that right, Dear?" He
nodded vigorously. "When I was six," she continued, "my
mother died. My father remarried and my stepmother hated
my sister and me. To make matters worse, I broke one of her
wedding presents and she hated me even more. My father

suggested I ask her forgiveness. I did and found that she not only wouldn't accept my apology but she hated me still more. I have never from that moment to this asked anyone's forgiveness.

"But at this conference I have discovered in the openness and the love that what I have heard in church all my life is true. I heard that God loves me as I am and believed it, but no one else has ever treated me as though he believed it. Now I know it's true; I am released and am even free to ask forgiveness when I am wrong." These are the kinds of miracles that should be taking place every day in every church — God working through ordinary people to bring release to others. This is normal Christianity.

A New Center of Authority. Each era has demanded a different center of authority through which God could confront the world. In the Dark Ages God used the very structure of the Church as the one organized, learned institution in a chaotic society. During the Reformation the Bible was rediscovered and became for Western Civilization the center of authority through which God spoke. Still later, preaching became God's primary means of confronting men.

But the world today is not impressed by the Bible, or by the Church, or by preaching. And we cannot confront a needy world with God's love primarily by these means. The climate of our time is one in which people listen most readily to laymen with whom they can identify. So as in the first century, ordinary laymen have become the center of spiritual authority.

Madison Avenue is discovering that the person down the street who is "just like me" is the person I will listen to. Much of our present-day advertising focuses on unknown women in laundromats, unknown truck drivers, or unknown students reporting the findings of dental tests.

A gifted pastor in South Dakota is much in demand as a speaker and evangelist. But he has discovered that teams of his own laymen going into other churches to witness are more effective in reaching people and aiding in renewal. These teams of laymen are not a schedule-stretcher for a busy parson, but actually a more generous and effective means of one church sharing its "new life" with other churches.

A New Language. Clinical reporting is a universal language in a way that concepts and theories are not. Truth can best be communicated not only to the pagan world but to other Christian groups if we stay on the level of experience.

If I talk about "sin" or "grace," I find great difficulty in communicating. But if I, as a father, talk about my failures in everyday living and about receiving a new kind of love from God for my children, I find that I am understood by the Christian and pagan father alike. We must learn to say, "Let me tell you what happened the other day," rather than, "I think this is what you should do." Clinical reporting is the language of the ecumenical movement at the grass roots.

A New Fellowship. God is helping His Church discover the reality of apostolic fellowship. The Church is meant to be a company of people as committed to one another as to Christ and to have, as in the first century, "all things in common." Worship on Sunday should grow out of a life shared during the week in small groups meeting for prayer, for nurture, and for encouragement in personal ministry.

Alcoholics Anonymous, which has its roots in the Church, is a good example of how God can use honest, open fellowship to bring people to reality and power, to keep them that way, and to help them reach out and share the good news with others in need.

A New Focus in Theology. Our generation has experienced a rebirth of Biblical theology and has recovered the fact that God's truth is revealed primarily in events rather than in concepts or systems or ideas.

God, in choosing the Hebrew people to be His first communicators to the world, chose a people whose language was not conceptual or philosophical. Hebrew is an action language which centers in verbs rather than adjectives, and the Bible is basically a chronicle of events rather than a handbook of principles or a systematic theology. So we must see the Bible as a record of what God has done and how man has responded.

If this is the nature of the Bible, it has profound implications for our witness today. Biblical preaching will stress the fact that God is acting now and will be illustrated with stories of present encounter. Truth is a living God speaking to a man and acting in his life. The substance of faith is man's obedience and action, which lays the groundwork for the new authority of lay witness.

A New Evangelism. The new evangelism differs from the old in manner, means, and approach. The emphasis is more on person-to-person relationships than mass meetings, on laymen witnessing rather than clergymen preaching, and on love as the motivation for response rather than fear and guilt. These were Jesus' own methods.

When we see how Jesus treated the Samaritan woman who was living in adultery, we are staggered. He honored her theological discussions and treated her with love and respect. The result was that she confessed her sins, bore witness, and brought the whole town to meet Him.

The same thing was true of the hated collaborator and tax collector, Zacchaeus. Jesus honored him with a visit, respected him as a person, and ate at his table. As a result Zacchaeus said,

"I'm a terrible person. I've lied and I've stolen, but I will repay it four times over and give half my goods to the poor."

The truth about God revealed in Jesus Christ is like a coin with two sides — love and judgment. Both are true. Many well-meaning people confront the world saying that life without Jesus Christ is hell and leads to destruction. But we are finding that most people are all too aware of their wrong-doing but cannot admit it until they discover the unconditional love of God. We are discovering Jesus' own method that the truest way to produce "conviction of sin" is to declare and demonstrate to people, "God loves you just the way you are."

A friend of mine in a weekly luncheon group in New York reported that God was giving him a new freedom with people. "I've always been sticky and pious," he explained, "and have been unable to say anything to strangers except 'Do you know the Lord?' The other day I watched a woman feeding pigeons in Bryant Park and began to pray for her. I felt prompted to say to her, 'You remind me of Albert Schweitzer.' She was visibly shocked and said that people had called her many things during her years of feeding pigeons but never anything like that. What did I mean?"

My friend explained that Albert Schweitzer, the famous missionary, had a reverence for all living things because of his love for God. After such a gracious introduction he was able to talk naturally with this woman about God and His love and they parted friends.

One of the best ways to demonstrate God's love is to listen to people. Psychologists say it is impossible to distinguish intense listening from love. To care about a person enough to hear what he is saying may do more initially to introduce him to Christ than to tell him all kinds of things about God or yourself.

Intense listening is a way of affirming that God cares for people and is helping them even before they are aware of it. I have talked with hundreds of people from all kinds of circumstances. Whenever I suggest that God has been talking to them for a long time, even the most "unspiritual" invariably responds, "Yes, God has been talking to me. How did you know?"

Once a young British woman had the privilege of having dinner with two prime ministers in the same week, first Gladstone, then Disraeli. When a friend asked her what they were like, she replied, "When I was with Mr. Gladstone, I thought I was with the smartest man in the whole world. But with Mr. Disraeli, I thought I must be the smartest person in the world."

A New Style of Life. In recent years most active Christians have been identified either as those concerned about a personal faith or those involved in relevant social action. But to think that we must make a choice is heresy. God is raising up a new kind of disciple with a new style of life who is as much at home on a picket line as he is at a prayer meeting.

Any kind of social action that does not challenge individual commitment will not penetrate to the core of the problem. But any kind of personal relationship with Christ which does not involve us with a suffering world for which Christ died, is certainly an affront to the very Lord who is in His world suffering with all people.

A New Understanding of the World. Too often we think that if we are children of God through spiritual rebirth, we will automatically be in the will of God for daily life. Nothing could be further from the truth. Unfortunately many who don't know God may really be deeply involved in some aspect of His work, while sincere Christians may be working at cross-purposes to His will.

A clergyman came into his study one morning to find his little daughter gluing the pages of his new manuscript together into a hopeless mess. "What are you doing?" he shouted. The little girl replied, "I am helping you, Daddy." How often God's children have messed up His work!

What freedom we have when we see that God is already at work in the world. We can co-operate with Him and perhaps interpret what He is doing to our fellow workers who may not be Christian.

Several years ago a Christian youth group in East Berlin gave their free time to join with a communist youth group in building an orphanage. When the communists asked the Christians why they were helping them, knowing that Christianity and communism were at cross-purposes, the Christians replied, "You are doing God's work in the world and we want to help you." The communists were furious! But think of the impact of this witness. The Christians did not say that being a communist was God's purpose but that caring for homeless children is always God's purpose in the world.

The Bishop of Toronto said recently, "God does not spend much time in church!" What amazing insight! We Christians must come to see that it is *the world* for which Jesus Christ died and that we who belong to Him by faith must enter into the world to redeem it and change it simply because it is His world, whether the world knows it or not.

GROUP

DISCUSSION

GUIDE

Bruce Larson has organized the material in this book for use
in group discussions. Seven major aspects of your life are out-
lined and cross-indexed by chapter and page to help you bring
more happiness and purpose to your family, your friends and
yourself.

GROUP DISCUSSION GUIDE

LESSON 1   Chapters 1-2

1. Man's Predicament.
    a. "Life is meant to be an adventure" is the first sentence in the book.
       Discuss: In what ways do you, or don't you, think of your life as an adventure? (Or is it more like a treadmill, a series of dilemmas, routine without purpose, etc?)
    b. How is your life affected by how you deal with the "basic issues" listed on page 13? Which of these are most basic to you at this point in your life?
2. God's Challenge.
   Pages 14 and following tell of the two obstacles to healing and release.
    a. Give some personal examples of this unwillingness to admit mistakes.
    b. In terms of this need for love, discuss:
       —how is the experience of Ruth like or unlike yours? (p. 20)
       —in what ways should your actions parallel those of the college student? (pp. 14, 17, 19)
3. In what ways might you find it difficult to believe what it says "Christians believe" in the last paragraph on page 32?
4. Did you find it difficult to discuss the subject matter today? If so, why? If not, why?

NOTES

LESSON 2   Chapter 3

1. "The home is the most difficult and most rewarding place for any Christian to put his faith to work." (p. 36) Would you be inclined to agree or disagree? Why?
2. Toward the bottom of page 37 is the statement about co-operating with God's purpose and plan for us. How does this concept strike you?
3. The four ways described.
   a. Let Him begin with you. What does this say about you in your home?
   b. How to love in God's way. Discuss what these mean:
      —being free to be vulnerable
      —give love in terms meaningful to others
      —giving undivided attention
   c. Honesty. Why is this so difficult?
   d. Let others minister to us. How might this be your problem?
4. "The situation is hopeless but not serious." Could this imply such notions as:
   —humor and humility are closely related
   relax and let God work in you
   —less struggle and more trust

NOTES

LESSON 3   Chapter 4

1. Discuss "love is not a technique that can be learned; it is a gift" and the remarks of Fromm following. (p. 50)
2. The four principles.

   In receiving

   a. Believe God loves us just as we are.

   Compare or contrast the ideas in this paragraph with your way of viewing His love.

   b. Be ourselves at all times.

   How might we go about expressing rather than repressing our hostile feelings?

   In transmitting

   a. Let others be themselves.

   Discuss the idea that our job is to love and God's job is to change.

   b. Believe in Christ's love for every person.

   Discuss ways in which you might channel His love.
3. "The greatest adventure in life is to experience the love of God in Jesus Christ and to transmit it to others." Can you say that? Why or why not?

NOTES

LESSON 4   Chapters 5-6

1. Discuss the idea "Christian truth is transmitted relationally rather than propositionally." (p. 57)
2. Chapter 5 lists five characteristics of dynamic relationships: identification, listening, personal honesty, vulnerability, willingness to receive.

   Discuss the meaning of any of these.

   Discuss your own feelings about them in terms of your own experiences.
3. Chapter 6 has five questions each of us should periodically ask ourselves about our job.

   Compare or contrast any of this material with your feelings about your job.

NOTES

LESSON 5   Chapters 7 and 8

1. Discuss some or all of these sentences in chapter 7.
   "No change in our circumstances is going to solve the basic problem in our marriage." (p. 76)
   "What is a Christian marriage? Basically it means that I can no longer do as I please." (p. 76)
   "A Christian marriage involves seeing and understanding the other person as he really is and loving him just that way." (p. 78)
   "There is no way for God to change a marriage and leave the people involved unchanged." (p. 79)
2. Chapter 8 says faith is composed of three ingredients.
   a. Faith in God and especially in the way He has revealed Himself in Christ.
      Discuss the difference in having faith in a principle vs. a person.
   b. Commitment that involves risk. Discuss the idea presented that this involves "specific and immediate implications." (p. 85)
   c. Hard work.
      Discuss what work may be required of you.
3. Discuss the quote from Butler on p. 87 about the three classes of people.

NOTES

LESSON 6   Chapters 9 and 10

1. Look at the second paragraph in chapter 9. Do you think it is true? Why?
2. Page 93 lists three steps to take in entering into a right relationship with God. Discuss your feelings about them.
3. Pages 93-96 has ten paragraphs on guideposts for effective prayer.
   Discuss as many of these as you find useful. Ask questions about them as well as share experiences and needs.
4. Chapter 10 is on praying together. Discuss why you might find this difficult: as husband and wife, as family, as friends.
5. Discuss the four points on making prayer alive in a group. (pp. 103-104)

NOTES

LESSON 7   Chapters 11-12

1. What did you find in chapter 11 that surprised you or caused you to wonder about your relationships to others? Discuss.

2. Chapter 12 lists ten facets of "God's strategy for today." Take any or all of these and discuss. You might want to consider:

   —is this an adequate and valid description or concern?

   —how does this compare or contrast with our congregation?

   —how does this speak to me and my attitudes and views?

3. What will be your part in the "church in revolution"?

NOTES